DIGITAL PHOTOJOURNALISM

DIGITAL PHOTOJOURNALISM

SUSAN C. ZAVOINA
University of North Texas

JOHN H. DAVIDSON
The Dallas Morning News

ALLYN AND BACON   Boston | London | Toronto | Sydney | Tokyo | Singapore

Series Editor: Molly Taylor
Editor-in-Chief, Social Sciences: Karen Hanson
Editorial Assistant: Michael Kish
Marketing Manager: Mandee Eckersley
Production Administrator: Beth Houston
Editorial-Production Service: Omegatype Typography, Inc.
Composition and Prepress Buyer: Linda Cox
Manufacturing Buyer: Julie McNeill
Cover Administrator: Kristina Mose-Libon
Electronic Composition: Omegatype Typography, Inc.

Between the time Website information is gathered and then published, it is not
unusual for some sites to have closed. Also, the transcription of URLs can result
in unintended typographical errors. The publisher would appreciate notification
where these occur so that they may be corrected in subsequent editions. Thank you.

Library of Congress Cataloging-in-Publication Data

Zavoina, Susan C.
    Digital photojournalism / Susan C. Zavoina, John H. Davidson.
        p. cm.
      ISBN 0-205-33240-4 (alk. paper)
      1. Photojournalism. 2. Image processing—Digital techniques. I. Davidson,
John H. II. Title.

TR820 .Z39 2002
070.4'9—dc21

                                                                    2001045703

Printed in the United States of America

10 9 8 7 6 5 4 3 2 1   06 05 04 03 02 01

Credits: Adobe and Photoshop are either registered trademarks or trademarks
of Adobe Systems Incorporated in the United States and/or other countries.

To Margie Duwe Collinsworth

The image . . . always has the last word.
—Roland Barthes

CONTENTS

PART ONE   TECHNOLOGY IN THE FIELD   1

CHAPTER 1

Scanning and Prepress Tools for Traditional Print Publications   1

CHAPTER 6

Photo Editing for Traditional Print Publications   73
By John Davidson, the Dallas Morning News

CHAPTER 7

Transmitting in the Field   117

CHAPTER 12

Case Studies and Ethics   159

List of Figures

Chapter 7

Chapter 8

Chapter 9

Chapter 10

Chapter 11

Chapter 12

CONTENT

Photojournalism is a language—a visual language. It is a process of communication—a very public form of communication. It is not always a pretty language, for the world we live in is not always a pretty place. Photojournalists document not only the good but also the bad and, at times, the ugly. They are storytellers—visual storytellers, the eyes of the reader.

We live in a time when people are more visually sophisticated than ever before. The mass production of images surrounds us. Anyone born after 1950 has grown up watching television and has been bombarded with images from a very early age. In addition to television, images appear in newspapers, magazines, books, billboards, and, more recently, on our computer screens.

The photographic image is perhaps the most powerful means of attracting readers to traditional print—newspapers and magazines. Photographs have the special power to give the reader an immediate, deeply felt insight into the news, generating an almost visceral response to an event or an individual.

Many news photographs have become cultural icons because of their impact and universal appeal. As such, these images define a particular event in an indelible manner and convey meaning that transcends the purely specific.

Consider, for example, the infamous image of the execution of a Viet Cong suspect taken by Eddie Adams during the Vietnam War. This is a visual record of one man's death during a war that took hundreds of thousands of lives. Today, over 30 years later, the photograph still speaks a timeless message about the brutality of war.

Among more recent examples are the poignant photographs of a fireman carrying the lifeless body of a baby out of the bombed Alfred E. Murrah Federal Building in Oklahoma City and the much publicized image of the heavily armed U.S. marshals snatching a terrified Elian Gonzalez from his relatives' home in Miami. These images will be forever linked in people's minds with the mere mention of these news events.

Similar to a textual narrative, photojournalism provides information and evokes an emotional response, but in addition, the photographic image generates an aesthetic appreciation for its composition and quality of light. These images put a human face on an event, adding emotion to the exploration of the human condition. An example of this is the image of 11-month-old Andrea being carried through a flood by her grandfather (see Figure P.1).

Photojournalism is an essential element in the mix of ingredients that make up newspapers and magazines—essential because of the inherent role in the presentation of the news but essential also for this simple reason: Readers like photographs and are drawn to them.

Research conducted by the Poynter Institute of Media Studies tells us that readership of photographs is higher than that of any other single element in newspapers and magazines. Typically, a photograph is the first element readers see on a newspaper page. Readership of stories and even headlines is greater when they are accompanied by photographs.

Tannie Shannon, 49, carries his granddaughter, Andrea, 11 months old, and his wife Florence, 51, holds the leash to Amadeus, the family's old English sheepdog, while evacuating their flooded home near Conroe, Texas. They have lived in the home for 21 years, and this is the first time it has flooded.

David Leeson, The *Dallas Morning News.*

Journalists cover an event with three "voices" of the print medium: narratives, informational graphics, and photographs. Which of these voices is most likely to be problematic?

It shouldn't be the narrative. That is written after the event. Even if a key moment is missed, information about it still can be obtained from other sources. The story can be edited until it is satisfactory.

The same is true for informational graphics. A graphic journalist recreates an event to illustrate a process or package vital information. Like the narrative, the graphic can be edited until it provides the desired information.

What about news photography? Unlike the narrative or informational graphic, its success or failure is decided in an instant—when the photojournalist either takes or fails to take the photograph that will tell an important truth about an event. If a wrong decision is made at the critical moment, or if no photographer is on the scene, one of the voices is weak or mute. No amount of editing can change that.

TECHNOLOGY

Today's photojournalists have experienced tremendous technological changes in the tools they use to practice their profession. A case study is David Leeson, an award-winning staff photojournalist at the *Dallas Morning News.* David has won two Robert F. Kennedy Photojournalism Awards, has been a Pulitzer Prize finalist four times, and has a reputation as one of the best journalists at his newspaper. He started his career in 1977 at the *Abilene Reporter News* using a large-format 2¼ camera before moving on to a 35mm camera a few years later.

In 1989, as a staff photographer for the *Dallas Morning News,* David covered the U.S. invasion of Panama. After processing the film in the bathroom of his hotel room, he sent photos back to Dallas each day using a drum scanner, the best technology of the day. Each color photograph took a minimum of 24–30 minutes to transmit back to the office.

Five years later, in South Africa, David covered the first elections after the fall of apartheid. Using a state-of-the-art scanner, he transmitted his photos back to the office in 6 minutes. Photojournalists from around the world lined up outside his hotel room, waiting to borrow the new technology.

In 1997, David covered a major news event in Corpus Christi, Texas. At the airport, waiting for his plane, he transmitted his photos back to the newspaper using a digital camera, a laptop PowerBook, and a cell phone. Each image took 3½ minutes to transmit.

More recently, while covering a late-night high school basketball game that pushed the newspaper's deadline, David transmitted a photo in 90 seconds. He did this from his car in the stadium parking lot using his cell phone, a G-3 laptop, and a Canon D2000 digital camera. Embracing technological advances, David is an example of a photojournalist who uses these new tools to deliver content—with an understanding that digital cameras, computers, scanners, cellular and satellite phones, and software are wonderful tools but that is all.

David says, "Motor drives, autofocus cameras, and lenses have allowed me the opportunity to concentrate more on the mechanics of recording a story on film. Recently, digital cameras have extended my deadlines, worldwide, by almost eliminating the extensive procedures once required to produce an image for publication." He adds, "Regardless of technology and change, the one element that has remained constant throughout my career has been the never-ending drive to find those poignant moments which could visually speak with fairness and accuracy" (see Figure P.2).

Content is the most important element of photojournalism. Readers usually aren't aware of the equipment, how hard a photographer works, or how long it takes to get the picture. They are interested only in the photographic image—if it is interesting and if has meaning to them.

As technology continues to evolve and photojournalists learn to use new tools, the impact of the still image will remain an important means of communication. Elements within a singular frame will continue to speak a universal visual language. What we hope won't change are the standard of ethics and the quality of content in the field of photojournalism.

J. D.

FIGURE P.2

In Huancayo, Peru, an Indian woman walks past a government soldier, who wears a ski mask to hide his identity from members of the Maoist rebel group Shining Path.

David Leeson, The *Dallas Morning News*.

HOW TO USE THIS BOOK

This book is designed as a text for photojournalism students. Familiarity with basic Photoshop and personal system calibration is assumed. However, step-by-step instruction is given on specific tasks that become everyday skills for photojournalists. Because most tutorials cover a comprehensive view of Photoshop, which includes many tasks suited for fine art and graphics use, this text was created to present only the information necessary for prepress and preweb publication of photojournalistic images.

Many photojournalism textbooks limit digital technology information and instruction to one or two chapters, and much of what is presented can be pulled from a plethora of other sources. However, this text puts it all together for the photojournalism student.

Many areas are covered briefly to give an overview of the information necessary to carry out the tasks for prepress handling of images. Technology has made scanning so easy that critical steps necessary for attaining proper density and for making color corrections are often overlooked. In Chapter 1, an emphasis is placed on explaining how to scan correctly.

ACKNOWLEDGMENTS

A book isn't written. It grows.

This book was helped by many along the way. Thanks to all the contributing authors and photojournalists. Many students will profit greatly from reading this text and seeing these images.

Our thanks to: Tom Kennedy, Keith Hitchens, John Long, John Pavlik, Alan Greth, Jon Freilich, David Leeson, Andrew Scott, Judy Walgren, Gayle Shomer, Todd Sumlin, Allison Smith, William Snyder, Ken Geiger, Arno Balzarini, Louis DeLuca, David Woo, Yuri Kochetkov, Joel Robine, Chris Gerald, Paula Nelson, Joe Stefanchik, Amy Smotherman, J. P. Beato, Barbara Davidson, Cheryl Diaz Meyer, Jim Mahoney, David McCreery, Vernon Bryant, Jeremy Enlow, and Emily Bryant.

For their input, support, encouragement, and consultation (and for answering e-mails) thanks to: Alex Burrows, Jim Gordon, Vin Alabiso, Joe Krakoviak, Paul Lester, Robert Ismert, Shane Bevel, Chip Somodevilla, Gary Barber, Ann Farrar, John Zack, Terrence James, Ken Kobre, Betsy Brill, Jean and Craig Trumbo, Brian Johnson, Meta Carstarphen, Cecelia Baldwin, Jim Albright, Tom Reichert, Jim Mueller, Nelia Smith, Rose Preston, Cori Ulrich, Susan Gilbert, and Maria Mann.

We would also like to thank the reviewers: Kim Bancroft, University of Georgia; Lelen Bourgoignie, University of Miami; John Freeman, University of Florida; Keith Graham, University of Montana.

Special thanks to Margie, Jan, Chase, Shea, and Goldie.

Digital Photojournalism

chapter **1**

SCANNING AND PREPRESS TOOLS FOR TRADITIONAL PRINT PUBLICATIONS

And so it goes: The magic moment of seeing the photographic image slowly appear on paper in the developing tray, from shadows to highlights, is no longer necessary. Some of us feel that something has been lost, but of course, something has also been gained. The speed and accuracy with which we can increase contrast, correct color, or adjust any element in the grammar of photojournalism by changing just one pixel in a digital image file make the digital method more efficient. As always in photojournalism, used correctly and ethically, the appropriate tools control the quality of the finished product.

Before the digital camera was developed, there had been little change in the photographic process that was perfected in the nineteenth century. A latent image is captured on silver halide crystals, developed, and then printed on photographic paper. By contrast, a digital camera captures light with sensors, and this is converted to a type of digitized latent image.

The same technology that is used in digital cameras is used in film scanners. By combining both worlds—photographic images recorded on film and digital technology—a hybrid system can be used to correct the image electronically. Instead of using your hands to dodge and burn and using enlarging filters to control contrast, computer software is used to prepare the photographic image for publication.

DIGITAL HYBRID SYSTEM

The 35mm film scanner is the foundation of the digital hybrid system that is currently used in most newspaper photo departments. The hybrid system is a working process combining analogue and digital information. Film (analogue information/continuous tone) is exposed, processed, and then scanned to create a digital image file. This system is used for prepress (traditional print) and preweb publishing.

The digital chain consists of image capture, image editing, and image output. Unless digital cameras are used for the image capture, the film scanner is used to convert the analogue image information into a digital image file. This first step of converting the film negative or positive to a digital file must be done correctly to have the digital information to produce a usable prepress image for output. The quality of the scan greatly affects the quality of the resulting printed image. It is important to make tonal adjustments in the preview scan, regardless of which type of film scanner is used, so that the quality of the scanned image is as close to output quality as possible.

FILM SCANNERS

Different types of film scanners are available. Currently, most newspapers use midrange or high-end scanners to scan 35mm negatives. Drum scanners represent the high end of scanning technology, while most 35mm film scanners are considered midrange. Scanning technology uses either photomultiplier tubes (PMT) or charged coupled devices (CCD) with filtration built into the chips to capture RGB (white light additive primary colors: red, green, and blue) values. This is similar to the analogue process, in which film emulsion is sensitive to and records white light primaries. Some types of scanners use filtration to automatically convert the captured RGB values to cyan, magenta, and yellow (subtractive primary colors). PMT devices and CCDs are discussed later in the chapter.

Drum Scanners

A drum scanner can be used to scan any film format size. The film is taped to the drum. As the drum rotates at a high speed, an inside light source travels across the film. The light transmitted by the film is measured by the PMT detector on the outside of the drum. PMT scanners are more sensitive than CCD scanners and are better at picking up detail in dark areas. Therefore, the highest possible dynamic range can be obtained from the object being scanned. Dynamic range is a measure of a scanner's ability to capture detail in the highlight and shadow areas of an image.

35mm Film Scanners

Midrange film scanners use a device that, like a light meter, produces an electrical output from the light that strikes each of its picture elements. Most midrange scanners are area array scanners, which capture the image information in one single exposure. (CCD and array scanning are discussed further in Chapter 3.)

When the scanner is positioned in a network configuration of an SCSI daisy chain, the SCSI ID number reflects its position in the chain of hardware. The scanner's external or internal terminator should be turned on when the scanner is the last device in the chain. The terminator acts as a stop sign to the flow of information to prevent signals from reflecting back after reaching the last device. If other SCSI devices are numbered after the scanner, the terminator should be turned off. However, it is always recommended that the scanner be the last device in the SCSI chain.

Although discontinued, the Kodak 2035 is one of the best midrange 35mm scanners. It is considered a workhorse for film scanning primarily because of the built-in film base information, which makes the scan more accurate. The Kodak RFS 3570 Plus is the new alternative. This is an area array scanner with a dynamic range of 12 bits per RGB color (exceeding 8 bits per color). Unlike these two Kodak scanners, the other frequently used 35mm scanners—the Nikon LS-2000, Nikon Super CoolScan II, and the Polaroid Sprint—do not give a choice of film base. Therefore, scanning from a Fuji negative will appear differently in the preview scan than when scanning a Kodak film base. However, the slight difference in color can be corrected in curves.

HOW TO SCAN AND DO PREPRESS STEPS IN PHOTOSHOP

Because software is continuously updated, these steps are described as generally as possible to be used with many versions of Photoshop.

After installing your scanner software, open the scanner software folder and drag the plug-in into the Photoshop Plug-ins Import/Export folder. Although scanning can be done with the software that comes with the scanner as a stand-alone process, this method allows you to scan directly into Photoshop. The scanner should be turned on before the computer is turned on. If necessary, clean the negative or positive with an antistatic cloth and/or canned air before placing the film into the scanner (see Figure 1.1).

WORKFLOW SUMMARY

- Scan preview: Set the film type/base, resolution, file size, and dimensions for crop. (More detailed information on resolution is given later in this chapter.)
- Adjust contrast, brightness, and color if necessary. (Using the factory defaults for contrast and brightness is recommended unless the negative or positive is not exposed correctly.)
- Scan.
- Save in appropriate file format for output/viewing.
- Caption the photo.
- After the scan, make adjustments, if necessary, in color and/or contrast, spotting, dodging, and burning.
- Save and also save a copy in RGB before converting to CMYK.
- Convert to CMYK.
- Unsharp mask at 100% view.
- Archive.

  Note: More detailed information is provided in the next section, "How to Scan 35mm Film Correctly."

FIGURE 1.1

Workflow Summary

How to Scan 35mm Film Correctly

To scan 35mm film, follow these steps:

1. Place the negative or slide with the emulsion away from the CCD. This is similar to placing the emulsion away from the light source in an enlarger. Depending on the configuration of the scanner, the emulsion may be "up" or "down." Most scanners have a film holder for negatives; slides are usually placed in the scanner without a holder.

2. Open the Photoshop program, go to the File menu, and select Import or Acquire, depending on the version of Photoshop you are using. Toggle to the scanner listed. If the scanner name is grayed out and not available, do the following:

- Make sure the scanner is turned on, quit Photoshop, and restart the computer or
- Check the SCSI number on the scanner and make sure it is not the same as any other device on the daisy chain or
- Make sure the scanner plug-in is in the Plug-Ins Import/Export folder in the Photoshop folder.

3. Click on the scanner's preview button to preview the image. (Note that the scanner viewing box will usually open with the image that was last scanned in the window.)

4. Set the film type. For example, select color positive for a slide, color negative for color negatives, and black and white negative for black and white negatives. (Black and white negatives may be scanned as grayscale or as a color negative. Reasons for choosing one or the other are discussed in the section on scanning specifically for black and white output.) If you are using a scanner that has film base option information for various brands of film types (e.g., Fuji 800 or Kodak Gold 400), set the film base.

5. Set the resolution according to your output needs: 72 ppi (or dpi) for screen use or approximately 200–300 ppi for traditional print output.

6. Set the dimensions to produce the appropriate file size. Be sure to lock the resolution and/or file size before adjusting the crop (see Figure 1.2).

7. If the contrast, tonal value, and color balance are adequate, scan. (Note: Instructions for various ways to balance color and adjust contrast and tone in Photoshop after the scan are given below.)

8. Save the image.

Captioning the Photo

Go to the File menu, select File Info, and a box will appear. In the caption box, type the date the photo was taken, the caption, and the byline, and name the file. (We will explain why this is important in Chapter 8, "Archiving Digital Image Files.")

Scanning Color Negatives or Positives

When the scan has been completed and the digital file appears on the screen in Photoshop, there are several ways to color balance the image for prepress

FIGURE 1.2

Setting Resolution and Image Size

SETTING RESOLUTION AND IMAGE SIZE

Scanning resolution is determined by output. If the scanned image is intended for web publication only, scan at 72 dpi (screen resolution). However, when scanning for traditional print output, printer (or press quality) line screen, printed image size, and paper stock should be considered. There are disagreements among professionals pertaining to scanning resolution in relation to these variables.

As a guideline:
The negative or positive should be scanned with a high enough resolution to render a good-quality image. Scanning at too high a resolution results in an unnecessarily large image size that will slow down the printing process and renders oversampling.

Based on a standard press line screen, scanning at a resolution between 200 and 250 dpi will result in a good print quality when outputting to newsprint. When outputting to a higher-quality paper stock, scan the negative or positive at 300 dpi.

Depending on the scanner being used, the location to set the parameters of resolution and dimensions will vary. Some professionals prefer to scan directly to layout size, and some prefer to scan to an open file size, and crop to fit the layout later in Photoshop.

Notes:
1. Some publications scan the negative or positive to the exact column dimensions needed for the layout (if that size has already been determined) at a resolution between 200 and 250 dpi.

2. Or set the file size in the scanner specification box to 6–8 megabytes and then crop later in Photoshop. However, make sure the resolution in the Photoshop crop tool option box is set to a resolution of 200–250 dpi with the fixed target box checked.

3. Keep the scanning resolution consistent for all images that will be printed in the same publication.

output. If the exposure of the film negative or positive is accurate, only minor adjustments will need to be made. (Corrections for negatives and positives that are underexposed or overexposed are discussed in Chapter 2.)

As a general rule, it is best to have an amount of **RAM** (random-access memory) three times the size of the digital file being edited. Virtual memory in the Memory submenu of the Control Panels menu should be turned off. Because of the reflective quality and dynamic range, color positives generally render a better scan from midrange film scanners than color negative film does.

Color Theory in a Nutshell

Color film is sensitive to the white light primaries: red, green, and blue. The subtractive primary colors—cyan, magenta, and yellow—are complements to the additive primaries. As in traditional color printing, color balancing of a digital

---

WHITE LIGHT PRIMARY COLORS

Additive Primary Colors   Subtractive Primary Colors

Red   Cyan

Green   Magenta

Blue   Yellow

*Adjacent colors are complementary colors.

FIGURE 1.3

White Light Primary Colors

image file is achieved by adding or subtracting the complements of each color or hue (see Figure 1.3).

The output format or use of the image determines the mode in which the scanned image should be color balanced: RGB or indexed color for web publications and CMYK for traditional print output. Most midrange 35mm scanners scan in RGB for color scans. Conversion to CMYK mode is done in Photoshop after the scan.

Modes

The mode of the digital image file is changed from RGB to CMYK in Photoshop by going to the Image menu and choosing Mode. However, if the image is going to be viewed online, the mode should remain as RGB or changed to indexed color (discussed in Chapter 4). Other mode options include grayscale, indexed color, CMYK, lab color, multichannel, and 8- to 16-bit channel options. There are differing opinions about when to change the mode from the original scanning mode of RGB to a traditional print output mode of CMYK. However, most agree that the mode change should occur before final color balancing is done in Photoshop, especially if custom color tables are being used. Specific instructions on when to convert and why are listed below and discussed in Chapter 2.

Converting to CMYK

When converting an image from RGB to CMYK, make a copy of the original image using the Duplicate command from the Image menu. CMYK is the color mode that is required to reproduce color photographs using printing presses. Because almost all color photographs for print media eventually must be converted to CMYK, convert RGB images to CMYK as soon as possible. There is disagreement among professionals as to the best time to convert an image from RGB to CMYK. However, by converting to CMYK early in the process, access is provided to CMYK channels in the Levels and Curves dialogue boxes. To prevent color degradation, do not convert back and forth from RGB to CMYK. Multiple conversions degenerate images owing to the rounding of color values when they are converted from one mode to another.

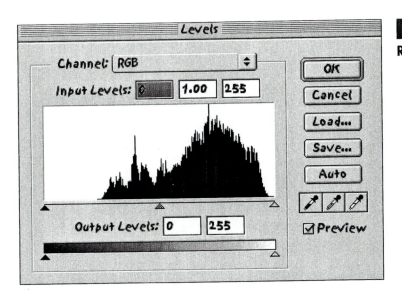

FIGURE 1.4

RGB Levels

Color Balancing and Setting Density in Levels

When the RGB image file is scanned and opened in Photoshop, do the following:

1. Go to the Image menu, select Adjust, and then select Levels (see Figure 1.4). Notice in the Channel listing that all three layers (RGB) are listed. Figure 1.4 represents a cross section or histogram of the exposure data. Notice that values 0–255 (total of 256) are listed. Zero is black; 255 is white. If the cross section of data does not extend all the way to 255, the image file does not have a true white point; and if the data does not extend all the way to 0, the image file does not have a true black point. Take note of the input and output numbers. A total of 256 values will be listed for each of the three layers (RGB) of the negative or positive. Never change the output numbers. Even after adjustments are made in Levels or Curves, the image file should contain a full tonal range of 0–255 values. The triangular sliders under the exposure histogram represent shadows, midtones, and highlights.

2. Toggle to the red channel first (see Figure 1.5). Do not change the output levels listed at 0–255, and do not move the triangles under the output levels.

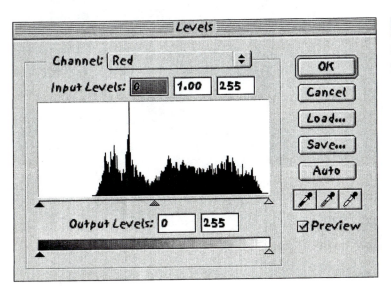

FIGURE 1.5

Levels, Red Channel

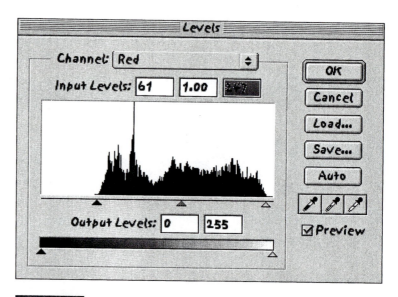

FIGURE 1.6

Levels, Red Channel Adjusted

3. Take the triangle on the left (shadows) directly under the cross section or histogram of the red channel, and click and drag to where the exposure data begins. Take the triangle on the right (highlights) directly under the histogram, and click and drag to where the exposure information begins (see Figure 1.6). Note the change in the input numbers but not the output numbers.

4. In the Channels list, toggle to the green channel, and do the same (see Figures 1.7 and 1.8).

5. Toggle to the blue channel, and do the same (see Figures 1.9 and 1.10).

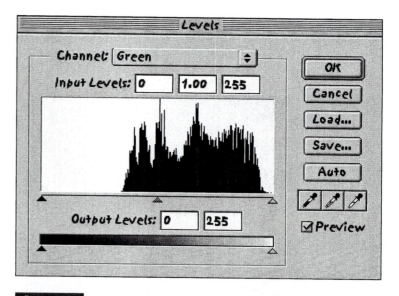

FIGURE 1.7

Levels, Green Channel

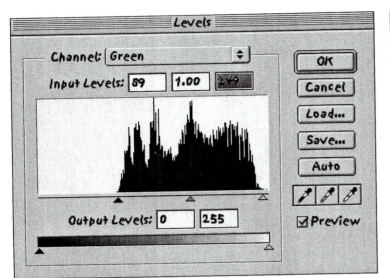

FIGURE 1.8

Levels, Green
Channel
Adjusted

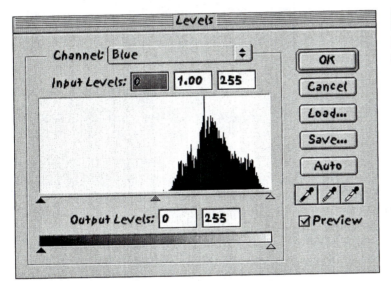

FIGURE 1.9

Levels, Blue
Channel

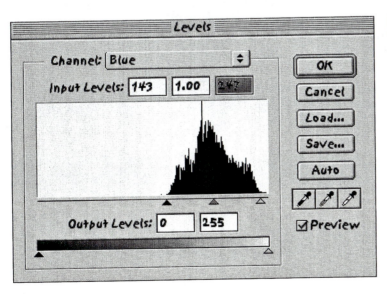

FIGURE 1.10

Levels, Blue
Channel
Adjusted

**Levels, RGB
Channel after
Adjustments**

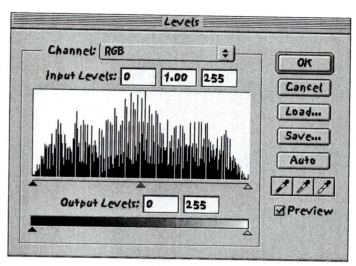

6. Toggle back to the first channel that contains all three (RGB), and look at the finished histogram (see Figure 1.11). Take note of the input and output levels. Notice that both contain the 0–255 levels needed for a full-range image file.

Color Balancing in Curves

In the Curves window, the data for the image file is plotted on a gamma curve graph with 0% representing white and 100% representing black. Make sure white is represented on the bar under the graph on the left side and black on the right. If not, click on the double arrows on the bar under the graph. Adjustments in Curves may be used to affect color balance and correct contrast similar to using levels. However, corrections made in Curves are considered to be slightly more precise because any number of specific points can be selected along the gamma, providing more control. The eyedropper in the Curves dialogue box can be used to set shadow, midtones, and highlight points.

To correct color in Curves, go to the Image menu, select Adjust, and then select Curves (see Figure 1.12). In Figure 1.12, curves are displayed for an RGB

Curves, RGB

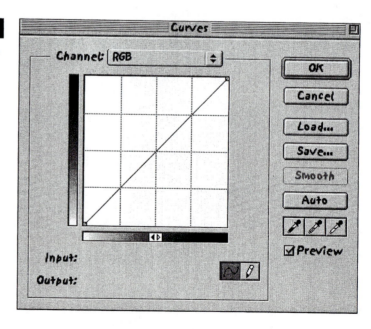

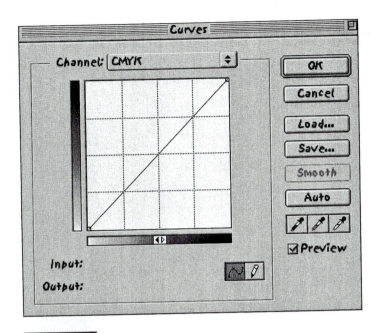

FIGURE 1.13

Curves, CMYK

image. Depending on the process that is used, color correction may be done in RGB curves or CMYK curves. Most professionals recommend converting to CMYK before color correcting in Curves (see Figure 1.13).

Figure 1.14 indicates which way to adjust the diagonal line to adjust density and contrast. As is stated above, these adjustments can also be made by clicking on the eyedroppers and selecting either black, white, or midtone in the image. Pure black is 100%, pure white is 0%, or numbers in the Info box can be set for a neutral midtone (see Figure 1.14).

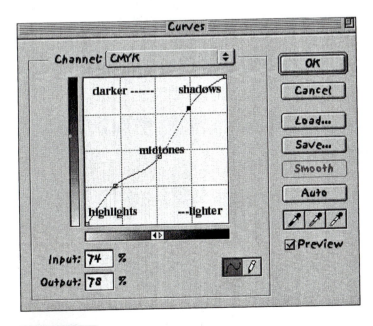

FIGURE 1.14

Curves

Curves, Cyan Channel

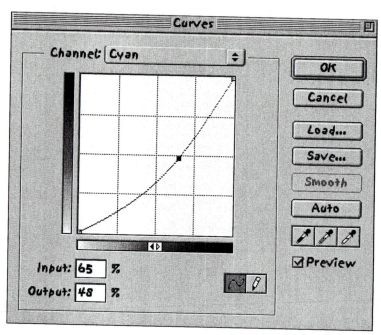

It is important to remember primaries and complements at all times when color balancing. When going to each CMYK channel individually in the Curves screen, moving the diagonal line at any point will either add or take away the complementary color. In Figure 1.15 in the cyan channel, where the line is moved down, red will be added. Where the line is moved up, red will be taken away, adding more cyan (see Figure 1.15).

Color Balancing in Color Balance

The Color Balance option in Photoshop is the most similar to color balancing in a color enlarger. However, color balancing in Curves or Levels provides more precise control.

To color balance in this option, go to the Image, select Adjust, then select Color Balance (see Figure 1.16). Subtractive primaries are listed adjacent to

FIGURE 1.16

Color Balance

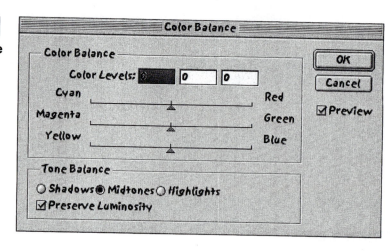

additive primaries, simplifying color theory. For example, if the image is too cyan, red is added. If the image is too magenta, green is added. This method of color balancing and the method in the Variations option described below provide the option to affect highlights, midtones, or shadows.

Color Balancing in Variations

This method of color balancing requires knowledge of additive primary and subtractive primary colors. To correct a specific hue, the operator must know which hue to add. As in the Color Balance option, this method is not as precise as the color correction process in Curves or Levels (see Figure 1.17).

1. Go to the Image menu, select Adjust, and then select Variations. Take note of the Original and Current Pick views of the image. These will show any changes. Also take note of the choices listed in the top right of shadows, midtones, and highlights and saturation.

2. Pick the area that needs to be color corrected: shadows, highlights, or midtones.

3. Adjust the color by adding the complementary color of the color that is too apparent. If the image is too magenta, add green; if the image is too blue, add yellow; and if the image is too red, add cyan.

4. Overall lightness and darkness can be adjusted in the windows on the right. However, a more accurate adjustment can be made by using Curves.

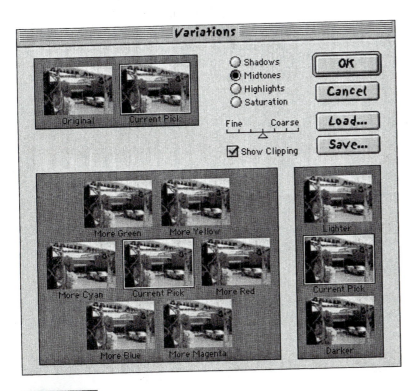

FIGURE 1.17

Variations

Photo by Vernon Bryant.

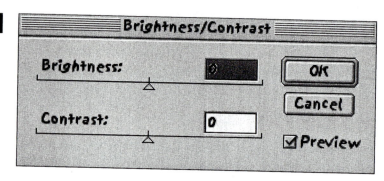

FIGURE 1.18

Brightness/
Contrast

Adjusting for Brightness and Contrast

Never adjust the brightness in the image file by using the Brightness/Contrast option (see Figure 1.18). Adjusting for brightness here compresses the tonal range of the image. The contrast adjustment may be used. However, it is best to make the adjustments in Curves.

Lightness/Darkness in Relation to Color

The lightness or darkness of a photograph can be adjusted by using the Lab Color mode without harming the color content of the image. Lab color is an international standard that color scientists use to describe colors mathematically. Colors are defined by using three channels: lightness, the A channel, and the B channel. Lightness refers to the lightness or darkness of a color; it contains only black and white data. The A channel contains color information and is a continuum ranging from magenta to green. The B channel is a color continuum ranging from yellow to blue. Lab Color mode is used as the intermediate system because it is device independent, creating consistent color output (see Figure 1.19).

Adjusting Saturation

Saturation is the percentage of color in the digital image file. Saturation values may range from 0 to 100% in Photoshop. When adjusting saturation, add only small amounts. Too great an adjustment will result in oversaturated images. Or if saturation is taken away, the image will appear "dirty" or more gray in traditional press print output (see Figure 1.20). (Correcting bad scans or exposure problems is discussed further in Chapter 2.)

Unsharp Masking

The Unsharp Mask option is a process that adjusts the pixel edge tonal range to give the illusion of a sharper image. There are three adjustment settings:

Amount: Controls the percentage of sharpening. The higher the percentage, the more sharpening is applied. It is not uncommon to use between 100% and 150%.

Radius: Controls the width or area where the sharpening will be applied. The greater the number, the more sharpening will occur. A recommended setting would be 2.

Threshold: Controls the change in tonal value of the pixels. The larger the number, the less change in contrast; 0 is the greatest contrast value change.

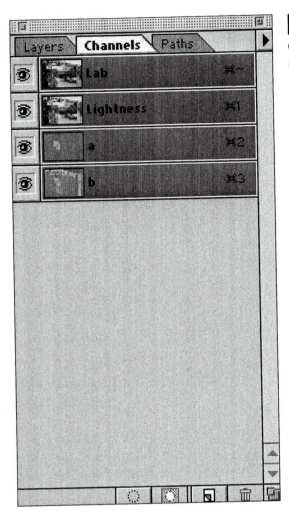

FIGURE 1.19

Channels

Photo by Vernon Bryant.

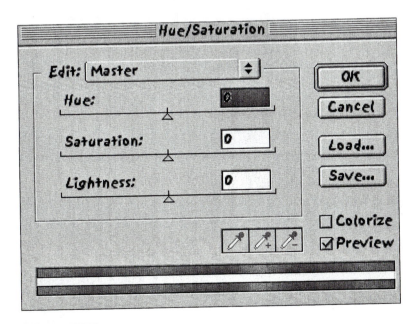

FIGURE 1.20

Hue Saturation

FIGURE 1.21

Unsharp Mask

Photo by Vernon Bryant.

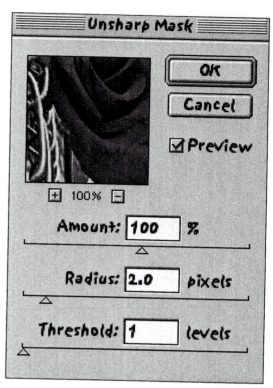

Unsharp masking may be applied to the entire image or to areas within the image selected with various selection tools. However, do not reapply unsharp masking to the entire image. Many professionals suggest applying unsharp masking in lab color (see Figure 1.21).

Dodging and Burning

There are various methods to dodge and burn an image. Ironically, the dodge and burn tools do not render the best dodge and burn tonal values. Either make a selection using the selection tools—the lasso or magic wand—or create a clipping path and change to a selection (described below) and then adjust tonal value in Levels or Curves.

Create a selection by using a clipping path:

1. Select the pen tool.
2. Outline the area to be burned or dodged. Small increments can be selected by clicking each necessary point.
3. Go to the menu bar, select Window, and then select Show Paths.
4. With the right arrow, toggle to make a selection.
5. A box will appear; choose New Selection.
6. Then toggle to turn off path.
7. Go to Levels to adjust highlights, shadows, or midtones.

Selection Tools in Photoshop

When the selection tools are used in Photoshop, only the areas that are selected will receive the applied changes. Different selection tools are applicable for different functions. Selection tools are the lasso, magic wand, and pen tools. Remember to double click on each tool to bring up the tool option menu. In most versions of Photoshop, holding down the shift key while using a selection tool will allow you to add to a selection, and holding down the option key will allow you to take away from a selection.

Using Quick Mask to Burn

A quick mask can be used to burn down a large bright area in an image.

1. Go to Quick Mask Mode near the bottom of the tool bar (see Figure 1.22). When this mode is selected, the words *Quick Mask* will appear in the title bar of the image.

2. Select the Gradient tool. Double click on the tool to bring up the gradient blend tool options, and make sure Linear Blend is selected.

3. Go to the foreground/background colors box on the tool bar and click the smallest foreground/background icon to set the default colors for the foreground and background.

4. With the Gradient tool selected, draw a blend in the quick mask layer. The area in the first click will not be selected, and the area of the last click (as you click and drag) will become the area selected when returning to standard mode from quick mask mode. So begin the gradient blend in the area that does not need the burn, and drag to the area that needs the burn.

5. Return to standard mode by clicking on the adjacent mode icon.

6. Note what area is encapsulated by the "marching ants." This is the area where the burn will be applied (see Figure 1.23).

FIGURE 1.22

Quick Mask Mode, Top Right

FIGURE 1.23

Selected Area to Be Burned in

Clusters of flowers were placed on a nearby fence in front of Wedgwood Baptist Church.

Photo by Vernon Bryant.

FIGURE 1.24

Redefined Selection of Area to Be Burned in

Photo by Vernon Bryant.

7. If there is something in this area that needs to be removed from the selection, click on the lasso tool and hold down the option key as you use the lasso tool to select the area of the selection that needs to be taken away (see Figure 1.24). Alternatively, hold down the shift key to add to the selection.

8. Go to the Image menu, select Adjust, select Curves, and raise the curve slightly to darken the area.

File Formats and Resolution

The output or use of the image determines the scanning resolution and which file format to use to save the image. Some programs will import (or open) only specific file formats. If the color negative or positive is scanned and edited for a traditional newspaper page, the standard file format is TIFF or EPS. Both of these file formats record color separation information. If the image is being edited for online viewing, standard file formats are GIF, JPEG, and PNG (discussed in Chapter 4).

TIFF (tagged image format file): TIFF uses LZW lossless compression (discussed in Chapter 4). This file format was created to standardize digital images for cross-platform desktop publishing. Both TIFF and EPS file formats are used to save color separation information. However, TIFF produces a smaller file than EPS does.

EPS (encapsulated PostScript): Almost all illustration and page layout programs support EPS. As was mentioned above, EPS file format records color separation information. This is the only file format that can save clipping paths and halftone screen information.

Scanning resolution is commonly specified in pixels per inch (ppi). However, resolution may also be expressed in dots per inch (dpi). The higher the resolution of the scan, the better the output image will be. Most newspapers scan to achieve an output resolution of 200–250 dpi and a screen resolution of 72 dpi for online publication.

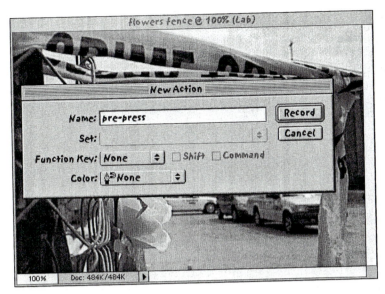

FIGURE 1.25

Dialogue Box to Title an Action for Recording

Photo by Vernon Bryant.

Putting It All in Actions

As a system of prepress steps is created, these can be recorded in actions to make the process more time efficient. This also establishes a standardized way of handling the images for more consistent output. For example, steps of setting levels, converting to CMYK, and unsharp masking can be recorded to operate automatically.

In Photoshop, go to the Window menu and select Show Actions to bring up the actions palette. Toggle the right arrow to New Action. A box will appear to title the action and record it (see Figure 1.25).

Apply all the prepress steps in the order to be executed, and then toggle the right arrow to stop recording. A "stop" can also be recorded in the process for a specific step to be done manually (see Figure 1.26).

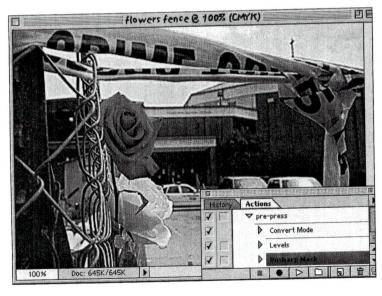

FIGURE 1.26

Example of Recording a "Stop" in Actions

Photo by Vernon Bryant.

What You Need to Know about Layers

Once an image has been scanned and is in Photoshop, most prepress corrections and changes will not involve creating layers. However, if a layer is created in editing an image, the layers must be flattened and merged before output. This is done by toggling the right arrow on the Layers menu and choosing Flatten Image and Merge Layers.

Scanning Specifically for Black and White Print Output

Color photographic images that have been converted to black and white usually appear flat and dull. Sometimes a better black and white reproduction can be achieved by using one of the color channels of an RGB or CMYK image rather than converting the entire photograph to grayscale. This can be done in the multichannel mode. This is discussed in Chapter 2.

However, scanning from a black and white negative can be done in grayscale or RGB mode. When scanning in grayscale, do the following:

1. Place the negative in the scanner as instructed earlier in the chapter.
2. Set the film type to grayscale/negative.
3. If contrast and brightness appear adequate in the preview, then scan.
4. To adjust the scanned image for highlight, shadows, and midtones, go to the Image menu, select Adjust-Levels, and slide the triangles in where the information begins (see Figures 1.27 and 1.28).

Alternative Method for Setting Contrast and Tone

To adjust the contrast and tone, you can do the following:

1. Go to the Image menu, select Adjust, select Levels, and double click on the eyedropper for the white point. When the color picker appears to set the white target, set C, M, and Y values to 0 and set the K (black) value to 5% (see Figure 1.29).

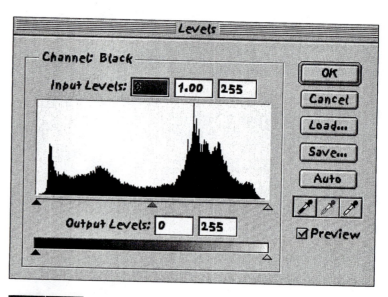

FIGURE 1.27

Levels, Black Channel

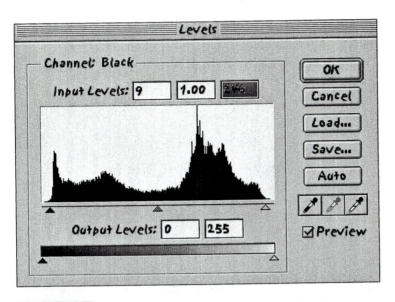

Levels, Black Channel Adjusted

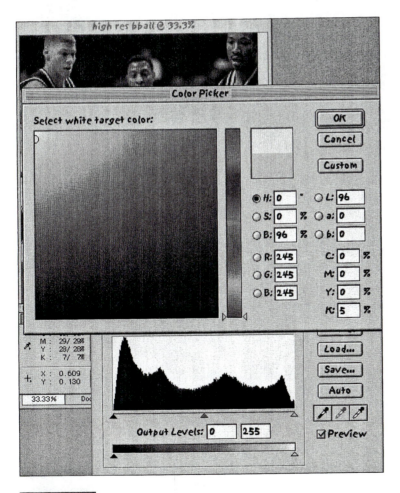

Setting the White Target

Photo by Vernon Bryant.

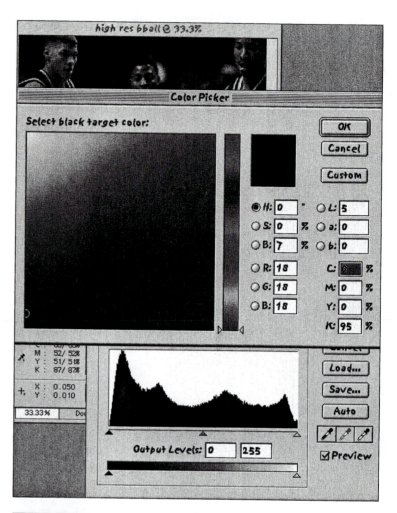

FIGURE 1.30

Setting the Black Point

Photo by Vernon Bryant.

2. Set the black point by double clicking on the black eyedropper, and set the C, M, and Y values to 0 and the K (black) value to 95% (see Figure 1.30).

3. Determine where the white point or highlight is in the image by going to the Image menu, selecting Adjust, and then selecting Levels. Hold the option key down, and click and slide the triangle to the left and then to the right to identify the highlight area. The areas that turn white first are the highlight or white point areas (see Figure 1.31).

4. Determine where the black point or shadows are by doing the same as above but with the triangle under the shadow information in Levels (see Figure 1.32).

- Click on the white point eyedropper, and click on the area of the image chosen as the highlight or "whitest" area.
- Click on the black eyedropper and click on the area of the image chosen as the shadow area.
- Adjust midtones in Levels by sliding the triangle to lighten if necessary (see Figure 1.33).

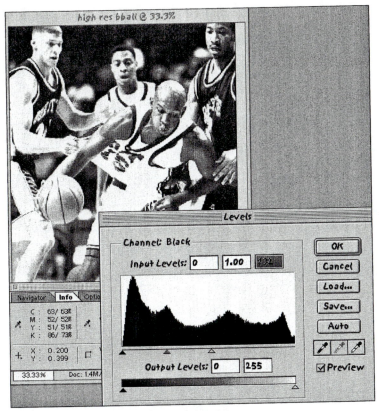

FIGURE 1.31

Highlight or White Point Areas

Reginald Erskin drives to escape the grasp of Roberto Bergersen and his teammate C. J. Williams of Boise State. The Broncos defeated the UNT Eagles in the end with a 78–71 victory. Erskin led the Eagles in points with 18.

Photo by Vernon Bryant.

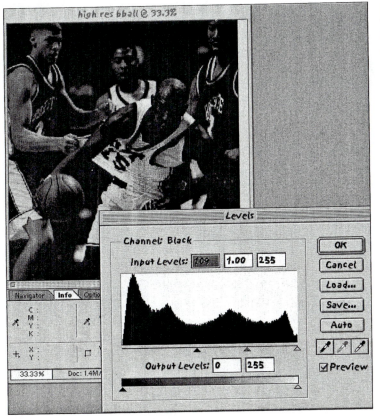

FIGURE 1.32

Determining the Black Point or Shadows

Photo by Vernon Bryant.

FIGURE 1.33

Adjust the Midtones by Sliding the Middle Triangle

Photo by Vernon Bryant.

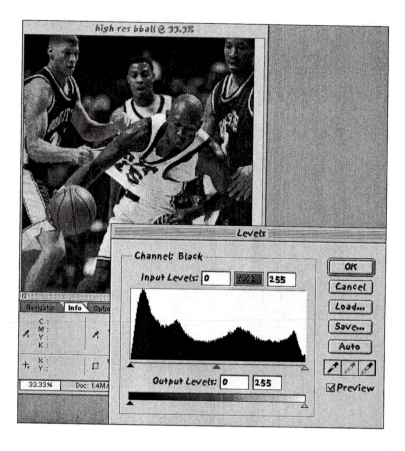

5. Apply the unsharp mask. (Note: When the highlight area is off by a small percentage, the eye perceives the change through either loss of detail in the highlight area or loss of contrast. There is more room for tolerance in the shadow area. If the shadow area is off by a small percentage, it is not as noticeable to the eye.

AREAS FOR DISCUSSION

- Compare and contrast adjusting the density and contrast of photographic images with traditional printing methods and with digital image files in software applications.
- Discuss the pros and cons of the various ways to color balance a digital image file and why one method might work better than another.

2

More Prepress Tools for Better Reproduction

Mies van der Rohe said, "Less is more." In using Photoshop (especially if the exposure of the image is adequate), that well-known adage really does apply.

The instructions listed below give a general overview of how to calibrate a computer monitor and the printing ink setups in Photoshop. Calibration is necessary for the printed output to have color, density, and brightness that closely resemble what is viewed onscreen when preparing an image for traditional print. Depending on the computer platform and the version of software being used, be sure to consult the computer and software instructions for more detailed information on calibrating your specific type of computer. Also, consult the book web site for updated information. Remember, even the type of room lighting (e.g., fluorescent or tungsten) will affect how the onscreen color is perceived.

CALIBRATION AND DOT GAIN FOR PRESS

For accurate color balancing, first calibrate your monitor using the Photoshop Gamma utility. To do this, go to your operating system's control panel and select Adobe Gamma. (On most types of Macintosh computers the Gamma setting is accessed in this way. However, for older or newer Macs, check in the Control Panel to see how to access Gamma settings.) Photoshop will prompt you through setting contrast, brightness, phosphors, gamma, and white point. Save these settings.

Photoshop Color Settings control how an image is displayed and affect how it is converted from RGB to CMYK for output. To set color settings, do the following:

1. Go to the File menu and select Color Settings (see Figure 2.1). (Note: This may vary with different versions of Photoshop. If you do not find Color Settings under the File menu, check the other menus.)

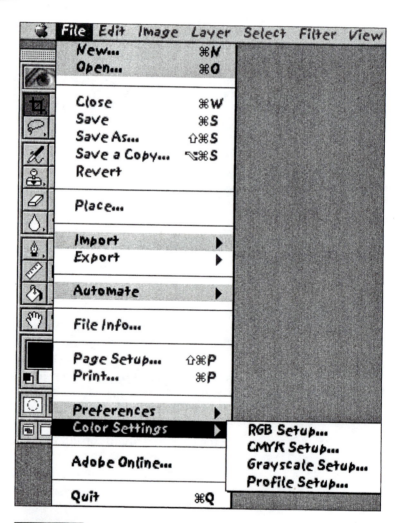

FIGURE 2.1

Color Settings

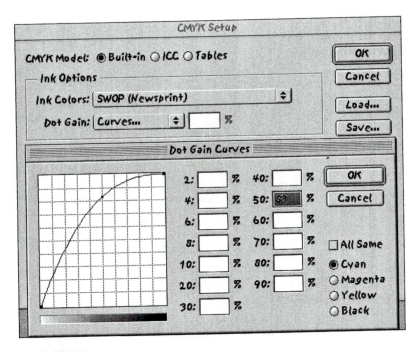

FIGURE 2.2

CMYK Setup for Ink Colors and Paper Type

2. Go to CMYK Setup (see Figure 2.2).
3. Set Ink Colors as SWOP (Newsprint) unless you know the specific type of press your publication will be printed on.
4. The dot gain for each CMYK channel can be adjusted by choosing Curves instead of Standard. These can be set accordingly to match press output. For most press output, the total black ink limit should not exceed 239%.
5. Next, go to Color Settings, select Grayscale Setup, and make sure the RGB radio button is selected under Grayscale Behavior 9 (see Figure 2.3). All of these settings are important when you are relying on the Info Palette values. Set your monitor desktop background as a neutral gray without patterns.

FIGURE 2.3

How to Set RGB for Grayscale Behavior

USING CUSTOM TABLES

Photoshop uses ICC profiles for one method of color management. An ICC profile is a color space description that has been defined by the International Color Consortium (ICC) as a cross-application standard. This is to help reproduce colors accurately across different platforms and applications.

However, custom tables can be developed to directly work with a specific press or printer (output).

Go to the Color Setting CMYK Setup and choose Tables to load custom CMYK color information. After this is loaded, the custom information will be used when CMYK conversions are made. The custom table overrides Photoshop's built-in color management.

USING THE INFO PALETTE

When color balancing or toning an image, it is important to understand the values in the Info Palette. No matter which method is used to color balance—Levels, Curves, Color Balance, or Variations—monitoring and understanding the Info Palette values will produce a consistent and accurate press output.

The Info Palette is similar to a densitometer, and the Printing Ink Setup values (instructions for setting above) affect the density of the image being color balanced. To access the Info Palette, go to the Window menu and select Show Info. Hold down the right arrow to bring up the Info Palette Options box (see Figures 2.4 and 2.5). Note that there are Mode and Ruler Units options.

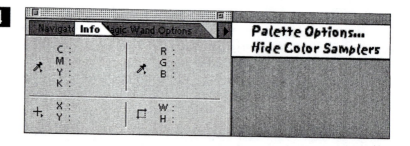

FIGURE 2.4

Palette Options

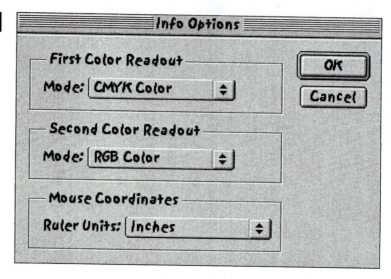

FIGURE 2.5

Info Options

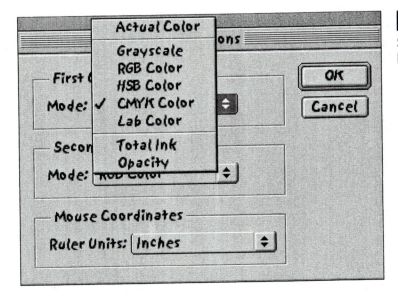

FIGURE 2.6

Setting Color Readout

FIGURE 2.7

Setting Color Mode in the Info Palette with the Eyedropper

Color and/or density values can be monitored in the Info Palette in actual color or in grayscale, RGB, HSB, CMYK, or lab color. Values of total ink and opacity can also be monitored this way (see Figure 2.6). These options can also be set by clicking and holding down the eyedropper in the Info Palette (see Figure 2.7).

Most professionals prefer monitoring Info Palette values in CMYK when monitoring values for press output. However, some professionals recommend monitoring values, especially skin tone, in grayscale even when the image will print in color. (More information on this method is given later in the chapter.)

On the basis of a standard setting for newsprint, total ink set at 239%, with CMYK ink set at factory default settings, recommended values for a good highlight skin tone in CMYK are approximately 5% cyan, 20% magenta, and 20% yellow for Caucasian skin and 25% cyan, 40% magenta, and 40% yellow for African or Latino skin.

When monitoring Info Palette values in grayscale, go to the Info Options dialogue box and set the first color readout to Grayscale and the second color readout to Total Ink.

When the eyedropper or crosshair is placed in the area that looks the blackest, it should read 239% for Total Ink Setup corresponding to the Total Ink Setup that was set when adjusting CMYK in the color settings (see Figures 2.8 and 2.9). The value to monitor is the K value. Figure 2.10 lists the recommended values for different skin tones.

FIGURE 2.8

K Value of Skin Tone of 35%

Zachary Gallatis with his "Little Engineer" hat.
Photo by Amy Smotherman.

FIGURE 2.9

Black Readout of 239%

Photo by Amy Smotherman.

RECOMMENDED INFO PALETTE PERCENTAGES FOR SKIN TONES IN GRAYSCALE		
Caucasian	25–55%	35% best
Asian	30–50%	45% best
Black	30–60%	60% best
Latino	25–60%	55% best

FIGURE 2.10

Skin Tone Percentages for Grayscale

COLOR CORRECTING UNDEREXPOSED OR OVEREXPOSED IMAGES

Although Photoshop should not be used to make very poorly exposed images look good, there are some steps to do this if the image has to be used.

Go to the Image menu, select Calculations, and then select Multiply. If the density is extremely bad, do the following:

1. Convert the photo to lab color mode.
2. Select the lightness channel in the Channel menu. This will temporarily convert the color image to black and white.
3. Correct the density by going to the Image menu and choosing Levels or Curves as discussed in Chapter 1.
4. Convert to CMYK mode.

COLOR CORRECTING FOR MIXED LIGHT SOURCES

When unfiltered fill-flash is mixed with fluorescent light, the background might have a green cast. To remove this, do the following:

1. Use one of the selection tools to select the green cast area. This will vary depending on the area that needs to be selected. The magic wand can be used if the green cast is in various areas of the background. Set the magic wand to the tolerance necessary (16 is recommended), and then hold down the shift key to add to the selection or the option key to take away. Alternatively, use the lasso tool to outline the area.
2. Go to the Image menu, choose Adjust, and then choose Hue/Saturation.
3. In the Hue/Saturation dialogue box, use the arrows in the Edit field to choose green (or whatever color might be needed to be taken out in another situation of mixed light, such as tungsten and daylight).
4. Use the eyedropper in the Hue/Saturation dialogue box to sample the green area.
5. Click on the Saturation triangle, and drag it all the way to the left to remove all of the green.
6. Click on the Lightness triangle, and drag it all the way to the right.
7. Click OK.

If there is another area in the image that is actually green and should not be altered, first select that area and then Inverse the selection so that it will not be affected by the steps above.

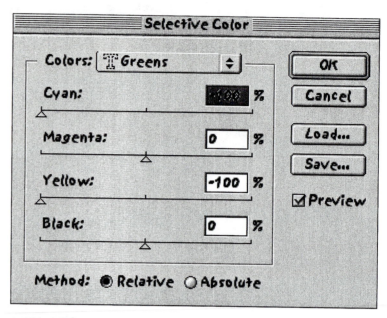

FIGURE 2.11

Removing Yellow and Cyan from Green in Selective Color

COLOR CORRECTING A GELLED FLASH SHOT

Another solution is to use a green filter on the flash and do the following:

1. Go to the Image menu, select Adjust, then select Selective Color, and choose Greens.
2. Remove yellow and cyan (see Figure 2.11).

CONVERTING TO CMYK FOR PRESS PUBLICATION

As was stated in Chapter 1, there is much disagreement about when to convert to CMYK color separation information when outputting to traditional print. This conversion splits the RGB into the three hues (adding black) for traditional print output. A good rule of thumb is to use the following method in Photoshop:

1. Preview the CMYK colors by going to Preview and selecting CMYK. To return to the RGB mode, reselect this option.
2. To monitor CMYK changes as editing is done in RGB, go to the View menu, select New View (to open a second window), turn on CMYK Preview in one window, and leave it off in the other.
3. Save a copy in RGB in case there is reason to reconvert.
4. Adjust for density and contrast in RGB mode using Levels by dragging the sliders to the parameter of the data.

5. Change to CMYK to color correct using Curves for each cyan, magenta, and yellow channel.
6. As was mentioned in Chapter 1, avoid switching back and forth from RGB and CMYK mode because each conversion requires reconfiguring the color and will result in less accurate color.

CREATING A BLACK AND WHITE CHANNEL FROM A COLOR IMAGE

When the color image will be printed as black and white, another option, instead of changing modes from color to grayscale, is to create a new channel. After the color negative or positive is scanned in RGB, do the following in Photoshop:

1. Go to the Image menu and choose Calculations.
2. Set the channel in source 1 to red.
3. Set the channel in source 2 to green.
4. Set the blending opacity to 50%.
5. Set the result to a new channel.
6. Click OK.

Alternatively, do the following:

1. Convert the image to lab color.
2. Throw away the A and B channels.
3. Convert to grayscale mode.

REMOVING NOISE FROM DIGITAL IMAGES

As is stated in Chapter 3, digital noise sometimes appears in images taken with digital cameras. Generally, the higher the ISO setting, or underexposure problems, the more noise there is. Most of this noise is usually in the blue channel. Various brands of software plug-ins and methods can be used to correct this, including Photoshop.

Quantum Mechanics is a Photoshop plug-in that most newspapers use to remove the noise without altering the color quality. Noise filters have a trade-off of randomly distributing pixels, affecting color quality slightly as the noise is removed. The downside is that using the filters may create an unusual texture. These steps can be applied to the entire image or to an image selection. Although most professionals working with prepress images prefer using the Quantum Mechanics filter to remove noise from the blue channel, noise and digital arti-facting can be removed, to some extent, in Photoshop. To remove noise in Photoshop, use either the Despeckle filter or the Dust & Scratches filter.

The Despeckle Filter

To use the Despeckle filter, go to the Filter menu, select Noise, and then select Despeckle. The Despeckle filter adds a blur to the image except for the edges.

The result is a "softening" of the image that preserves edge detail. Do this *before* applying the Unsharp Mask filter. Try various combinations of radius and threshold settings.

The Dust and Scratches Filter

As was stated above, remember there is a trade-off between image "softening," color quality, and noise reduction. It is important to vary the combination of radius and threshold within the Unsharp Mask filter to compensate for this.

To use the Dust and Scratches filter, do the following:

1. Go to the Filter menu, select Noise, and then select Dust & Scratches.
2. Drag the Threshold slider left to 0 to turn off the value. The Threshold slider gives greater control for values between 0 and 128.
3. Drag the Radius slider left or right, or enter a value in the text box from 1 to 16 pixels. The Radius slider determines how far the filter searches for differences among pixels.
4. Click OK.

The Median Filter

The Median filter reduces noise in an image by blending the brightness of pixels within a selection. The filter searches the radius of a pixel selection for pixels of similar brightness. Pixels that differ too much from the brightness value of the searched pixel are discarded.

To use the Median filter, go to the Filter menu, select Noise, select Median, and set the radius accordingly.

EMBEDDING A WATERMARK

A digital watermark can be embedded by using Photoshop to substantiate copyright protection. The Digimarc technology is a watermark digital code that adds noise to the image. This watermark works in digital and traditional printed forms. If an image that has an embedded watermark through Digimarc-Photoshop is copied, the watermark and information associated with it are retained.

Watermarking should be done at the end of the workflow of prepress or preweb publication. This should be done just before compressing the file (if necessary). Color variation may be affected, and the Digimarc technology requires a minimum number of pixels (but no maximum) to work.

The following dimensions are recommended:

■ When using a Digimarc watermark with a JPEG file format, make sure the image quality is set at 4 or higher when saving the image as a JPEG file. It is also recommended that you use the watermark Durability setting (which is explained later in the chapter).
■ Use 100 pixels by 100 pixels if the image will not be modified or compressed before its actual use.

- Use 256 pixels by 256 pixels if the image will be cropped, rotated, compressed, or modified after watermarking.
- Use 750 pixels by 750 pixels, or 2.5 inches by 2.5 inches, if the image will appear printed as 300 dpi or greater.
- There is no maximum limit on pixel dimensions for watermarking.

Note: Registration with Digimarc Corporation is necessary to use the watermark.

To embed a watermark, do the following:

1. Open the image. If working with a layered image, flatten the image before marking it.
2. Go to the Filter menu, select Digimarc, and select Embed Watermark.
3. If using the filter for the first time, click the Personalize button. A Creator ID will be issued by clicking Register. This ID will be needed to enter in the new Creator ID option.
4. Enter the copyright year for the image.
5. If necessary, select Restricted Use to limit the use of the image.
6. Specify whether the image is intended for traditional print or online publication.
7. Drag the slider or enter a value for watermark durability.
8. Select Verify to check the watermark's durability after it is embedded.
9. Click OK.

Note: When adding a watermark to an indexed-color image, first convert the image to RGB mode, embed the watermark, and then convert the image back to indexed-color mode.

The default watermark durability setting is designed to strike a balance between watermark durability and visibility in most images. However, you can adjust the watermark durability to suit the needs of your publication. Low values are less visible in an image but less durable and may be damaged by applying filters or by performing some image-editing operations, printing, and scanning operations. High values are more durable but may display some visible noise in the image. The setting should depend on the output and of the image. Check the signal strength meter before publishing the images.

To check the signal strength meter, go to the Filter menu, select Digimarc, and then select Read Watermark; the signal strength meter will appear at the bottom of the dialogue box. This can also be accessed by selecting Verify while embedding the watermark.

THE ELEMENT OF TIME

It is best to develop a standard procedure and workflow for adjusting color and density to streamline the prepress process. As was mentioned in Chapter 1, this way the process can be recorded in Actions, along with pauses or stops to allow for custom tweaking. Because there are many ways to perform the same tasks in Photoshop, decide which tools and functions work best for your purposes, and tailor the prepress process to fit the skills of the operators.

AREAS FOR DISCUSSION

■ Discuss various reasons to color balance in either RBG or CMYK.

■ Discuss the reasons why a photojournalist and/or a news publication would need to watermark an image. (See also Chapters 11 and 12 for more discussion of this issue.)

■ Create a customized streamlined procedure for preparing digital image files for publication.

chapter **3**

DIGITAL CAMERAS

As technology continues to develop at a rapid pace, new digital cameras will be less expensive and have higher resolutions approaching film quality. The web site that accompanies this book will update information as necessary. This chapter gives an overview of what was being used professionally in 2000.

When working in the hybrid system described in Chapter 1, the actual image capture is when the film (analogue information) is scanned. When a digital camera is used for capture, the image is also first recorded as analogue (in the camera) and then converted to digital information immediately (see Figure 3.1).

In theory, the digital chain is composed of

- Image capture: digital camera or scanner
- Image editing: editing software
- Image output: traditional print or online publishing

FIGURE 3.1

The Digital Chain

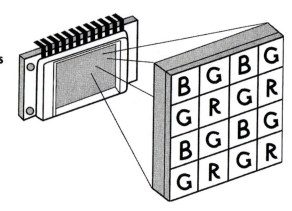

FIGURE 3.2

CCD Grid Panel Array with Additive Primary Coated Filters

Illustration by Emily Bryant.

WHAT A DIGITAL CAMERA IS IN A NUTSHELL

Most digital cameras are based on CCD (charge coupled devices) technology (discussed in Chapter 1). Instead of film, the image is focused on a grid of light-sensitive CCD sensors. Each sensor creates a voltage that varies with the amount of light received. The CCD diodes discharge light values and pass the signal from one diode to the next. The CCDs are arranged in a matrix array, and each element creates a pixel in the captured image. Digital camera resolution is based on the overall dimensions of the pixel array.

There are two types of CCD array formats: area array and linear array. In a linear array, CCD elements are lined up in a single row, and the image is scanned line by line. This linear sensor system is limited to use in some studio cameras and in certain types of film and flatbad scanners.

In an area array, CCD elements are arranged in a matrix that captures an image in one exposure. Therefore, image file resolution depends on the size of the CCD array (see Figure 3.2).

Similar to a film base that is sensitive to white light color primaries, CCD elements are coated with either red, green, or blue to produce the resulting color image file. In some cameras a red, green, and blue color filter layer is sandwiched with the CCD array. This matrix array is also called a *block array* or *block sensor* and is the type of CCD grid used in most professional digital cameras.

Another type of chip other than the CCD that is used in digital cameras is a complementary metal oxide semiconductor (CMOS). This technology is less expensive and the voltage conversion is faster than with a CCD grid. A smaller amount of power is used for the voltage conversion, but more noise may occur than with CCD technology.

CAMERAS BEING USED IN THE FIELD

Most of the favored high-end cameras for professional photojournalism are the digital cameras made by Canon and Nikon, in which 35mm single lens reflex camera bodies are coupled with the CCD chip panel or CMOS technology. Some older models were made by Canon and Nikon in conjunction with Kodak. Although cameras such as the Nikon D1 and the Canon D30 are adequate for press shooting, some of the older digital cameras have the closest CCD panel (resolution) that approaches film quality. The Nikon DCS 660 and Canon DCS 560 both have resolutions of 6 million pixels, whereas the Canon D30 has a resolution of 3 million pixels and the Nikon D1 has 2.75 million pixels.

Digital features and operating instructions listed below are somewhat general but are based on both the Nikon and Canon models. Most high-end digital cameras will have most features and operations that are similar. The list does not include all the bells and whistles that may be included in digital cameras. However, this is a quick-start list to familiarize the novice with a digital camera. For information on new cameras and updated instructions, go to the book web site.

FEATURES TO CONSIDER

Resolution

As was stated above, the size of the CCD grid panel establishes the resolution of the camera. The larger the CCD array, the greater the resolution. In lists of camera specifications, this size is translated to number of pixels. Currently, medium-range to high-end cameras have pixel numbers ranging from 2,008 × 1,504 (2 million) to 3,040 × 2,008 (6 million). For professional use, it is not recommended to use a digital camera with a resolution lower than the minimum listed above.

Changes in Focal Length of Lenses

In digital cameras the CCD grid panel is smaller than the area of a 35mm film frame (see Figure 3.3). As technology develops the size of the CCD grid panel may increase. Some panels are as large as 20.5 × 16.4 mm.

This size difference increases the focal length of the lenses used. A standard lens becomes a telephoto, and a wide-angle lens becomes standard. However, this varies from camera to camera and is based on the size of the CCD panel. (Check the book web site for updated camera specifications.) Most variances in focal lengths are increases ranging from 1.3 to 1.9, meaning that a 50 mm lens would be the equivalent of a 95mm lens. This might be beneficial in shooting sports, but it could be a hindrance in other shooting situations.

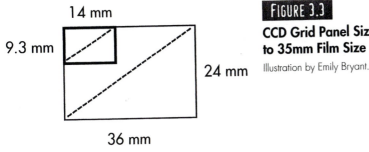

14 mm

9.3 mm

24 mm

36 mm

FIGURE 3.3

CCD Grid Panel Size Compared to 35mm Film Size

Illustration by Emily Bryant.

Interchangeable Lenses

Most medium-range to high-end digital cameras are made to use the same brand of lenses as that of the camera body. Use these lenses to ensure correct metering and to cut down on digital artifacting in the image (discussed below).

Anti-Aliasing Filters

Positioned just behind the lens mount, anti-aliasing filters are found only in most high-end professional digital cameras. The filter optimizes the light before it hits the CCD panel, cutting down on artifacting (multicolored highlights and patterns) within the digital image. The filter makes the light register more precisely on individual pixels in the CCD panel. There is a slight loss of sharpness, but most professionals agree that the trade-off is worth it. The loss of sharpness can be corrected by using Photoshop's unsharp mask.

File Size

File sizes for images produced from digital cameras are measured in megabytes. A camera with a 2 million pixel resolution can produce an image file size up to 5.7 megabytes. A camera with a 6 million pixel resolution can produce an image file size up to 18 megabytes.

ISO Range

Most high-end digital cameras have an ISO range from 200 to 1600. The ISO can be changed for each frame. This allows shooting to be tailored frame by frame for each shooting situation. However, the higher the ISO, the lower the image quality. Most professionals recommend using an ISO of 200 as the maximum. Noise in the blue channel increases with ISO. However, software such as Quantum Mechanics and Photoshop can be used to remove this (discussed in Chapter 2).

Image Storing/PC Memory Cards

Images shot in digital cameras are stored on PC (PhotoCards) cards, which are like small removable hard disks. These cards are about the size of a credit card and vary in storage capacity and durability. The three types of cards are type I, type II, and type III. Type I cards are not used in digital cameras because they lack the space to store digital images. Types II and III vary in thickness and storage capacity.

Type II cards, called Flash RAM cards, contain memory chips that resemble the RAM in a computer. Type III cards write data to a miniature hard drive.

There is a difference between cards with movable storage and those without movable parts. All cards are sensitive to severe changes in temperature and should be handled with care. Older models of cards are DOS based and must be formatted accordingly. Based on a 520-megabyte PC card, most high-end digital cameras can store 80–250 images on a type II or type III card. This is an approximation. Storage capacity is directly related to price. Any sound (WAV files) recorded will also take up storage space. These cards are essentially memory cards and must be installed when the camera is turned off. Different cameras take different cards. Most professional camera models use Smart Media or Compact Flash cards.

Burst Rate/Frames per Second

This varies considerably among high-end digital cameras. Older models range from 1 to 3.5 frames per second rendering 3 to 12 frames. Currently, the high-end professional cameras expose 3 to 5 frames per second rendering up to 40 frames. This is a factor to be considered, especially when shooting sports.

File Format

Early digital camera models employ Kodak's proprietary file format, which stores the thumbnail image as a TIFF that opens as a Photoshop file. However, once the image is opened in Photoshop, the file format can be changed. Cameras such as Nikon D1 can store the image data as raw data, TIFF, or JPEG. The type of image acquire, export, or download software used to transfer and view the images on the computer will dictate the best file format to use. Some software applications or application plug-ins work better using certain formats such as JPEG.

Color Depth

All of the DCS professional digital cameras have 12 bits per RGB color for a total of 36-bit color. A bit is the smallest unit of information that can be recorded. Bit depth refers to the number of bits per CCD (for capture) and pixel (for display).

Batteries

Most high-end digital cameras use removable, rechargeable NiCD batteries. These batteries must be properly maintained by using the conditioning and recharging methods recommended by the camera and battery manufacturer.

Interface/Connecting to the Computer

Because most laptops have slots for reading PC cards, connecting to a computer is not always an issue. However, when it is necessary to connect to a computer, an IEEE 1394 (or FireWire) cable is used to download the images. Unlike using a SCSI device, the computer does not have to be turned off before connecting the FireWire cable. Macs made before January 1999 will require an additional card for the computer to use this system. Remember to have the correct acquire software to view the images.

White Balance

All high-end digital cameras have a white balance setting (discussed below).

LCD Display

Built-in LCD displays allow for image proofing and can be used to determine exposure accuracy (discussed below).

E-TTL and/or Strobe Capability

Using a flash or strobe with digital camera systems has improved and is not quite the trial-and-error process it used to be. Portable strobes have now been developed to work specifically with the CCD panel. TTL (through the lens) flash to camera metering involves reading the light reflected off of a film base, not a CCD panel. When TTL is used with a digital camera, the result will differ from that of using TTL with film-based cameras.

Because standard TTL does not work the same way with digital cameras as it does with film, Canon and Nikon solved the flash/camera metering system differently. Currently, the Canon EX line of strobes use E-TTL and work with the DCS 520. E-TTL (evaluative through the lens) flash reads ambient light in combination with a preflash bounced off of the subject to determine the proper flash output. Nikon and Kodak's solution to incompatibility of TTL and a CCD array was to design the SB-28D, a version of the SB-28, to work with the DCS 620. When attached, the SB-28D automatically sets on auto aperture mode, which works best with the DCS 620 and AF and AI-P Nikon lenses. The Nikon Speedlight SB-28DX works with the Nikon D1 and features 3D multi-sensor balanced fill-flash. (Exposing with flash is discussed later in the chapter, and color correcting insufficient fill-flash is discussed in Chapter 2.)

Sound

All high-end digital cameras have sound-recording capability (discussed below).

OPERATING A DIGITAL CAMERA

Similar to acquiring scanner images through Photoshop (discussed in Chapter 4), the digital camera will have a plug-in that must be installed in the Plug-Ins Import/Export folder. (Alternatively, other software can be used.) Once this is installed, the digital images can be opened by opening Photoshop and going to the File menu, selecting Import, and scrolling down to the digital camera listed. If the digital camera is listed but is in gray, make sure the plug-in is in the correct folder.

Getting Started

These are the basic steps in using a digital camera for the first time:

1. Load the battery. It is recommended that you do this while the camera is turned off. If the battery is loaded while the camera is on, the camera might lock up, requiring the battery to be removed and reinserted.
2. Insert the PC or memory storage card. Check to see whether the particular camera being used should be turned off during this function. This will

vary depending on the camera being used. Most models require the camera to be off. The LCD panel will count down as images are taken. The card can be removed at any time except when the Card Busy light is blinking.

3. Turn the camera on, and confirm that the batteries are fully charged.

4. Press and release the Display or Monitor button to turn the image LCD display on.

5. In earlier DCS models a folder (FOLDER01) is created automatically when the PC card is inserted. Images will be saved to this folder by default. You can override this in the Select Folder menu. If a folder is created on the PC card, name the folder with a maximum of eight characters. The operating system is DOS-based and recognizes file names of eight characters or fewer. Newer models such as Nikon D1 do not require creating a folder. The images are stored one-by-one and can be deleted as you go.

Metering

The metering systems in digital cameras are the same as the camera bodies/systems the camera is built on. Most professionals suggest using evaluative or matrix metering (see Figures 3.4 and 3.5).

There is very little latitude, if any, for exposure problems when shooting digitally. Overexposure by half a stop results in loss of highlight detail, and underexposure results in noise. Most professionals recommend keeping the highlights, midtones, and shadows within a five-stop range.

In early DCS models you can view the histogram on the LCD panel after capturing the image. This will help to set the proper exposure for the lighting situation. Or, in newer models, if using the camera in manual mode, check your exposure on the meter.

The **DCS 520** is a Canon EOS1 camera body with evaluative metering, partial metering, and spot metering. Although four of the standard sixteen zones metered in the evaluative metering mode are outside the viewing area of the digital camera, this mode renders a correct exposure.

The **DCS 620,** an F5 camera body, employs matrix, center-weighted, and spot metering. The DCS 620's matrix mode is a 3D color matrix metering system that is compatible with D series lenses. If other lenses are used, the camera automatically sets itself to the center-weighted metering mode.

FIGURE 3.4

DCS 520 and 620 Information

The **Nikon D1,** similar to the N90 camera body, has 3D color matrix, variable center-weighted, and variable spot metering. Shutter speeds range from 30 seconds to 1/16,000 of a second. The TTL (through the lens) flash sync speed is up to 1/500 second.

FIGURE 3.5

Nikon D1 Information

The Ultimate Challenge of Capturing Color Correctly

Color balance preset selections are auto, daylight, tungsten, fluorescent, and flash. Most professionals prefer these preset selections to the custom selection. The daylight and flash preset selections are identical. Auto determines the preset necessary based on the lighting situation. When shooting in daylight only, use the daylight setting.

For custom color setting of neutral point when shooting in mixed light sources, choose the custom white balance and shoot the first frame of the assignment off the white or gray side of a card. Continue shooting. Before opening the images, set a click balance off the side of the card you used for the first frame.

ISO

As was stated previously in this chapter, most digital cameras will have an ISO setting range from 200 to 1600. Most professionals agree that setting the ISO on 200 renders the highest-quality image. To set the ISO on the DCS 520, hold down the AF Mode Selector and Metering Mode Selector buttons simultaneously, then turn the main dial. To set the ISO on the DCS 620, hold down the ISO button and turn the main command dial. To set the ISO on the Nikon D1, select ISO on the bottom menu and toggle the switch to the appropriate number.

Setting Custom Functions on Early DCS Models

The DCS 520 has fourteen custom functions that can be set from the Properties menu. The DCS 620 has twenty-four settings that are not available from the Properties menu but can be reached through the main control dial. (The settings will vary depending on the camera body.)

Using Flash

Always make sure the flash is off when connecting it to the camera. Take note of extremes in contrast and mixed lighting, even considering fill-flash (some of this is covered in Chapter 2). For best results use the dedicated flash made by the same company as the camera model. Newer professional digital camera models such as the Nikon D1, when used with the Nikon speedlight SB-28DX, will allow for TTL metering.

Set the appropriate color balance selection on the camera, usually the flash or automatic settings on the newer models. Results will vary when using the flash if the camera's color balance setting is set on other options.

Recording Sound Clips

Record caption information immediately after shooting if possible. If this is not possible, scroll on the LCD panel to the image and record the sound file. The sound file is a WAV file format (.wav) and is time stamped when you record it. The WAV file is not incorporated into the image file. Approximately 4 minutes of sound will equal the disk space of one image file.

Framing the Image

Crop tight because every pixel counts. As in filling the frame when shooting with film so that the main subject is not just a fraction of the film plane, make sure the CCD area (or the area of capture) contains a large area of the main subject. In other words, capture with a large figure–ground relationship in mind.

Reviewing Images In-Camera

This will vary depending on the camera being used. However, most digital cameras will allow the image to be viewed immediately after being captured. This allows for metering corrections to be made while photographing under the same lighting conditions. The term *chimping* has been coined to describe the "ooh, ooh!" expression photographers have as they glance down to view the image immediately. The immediacy is still novel.

Deleting Images

Images can be deleted in-camera either one at a time or in a group, or the entire card can be wiped clean. The method will vary depending on the digital camera being used but is similar to deleting images from any type of digital grid or file. Most digital cameras have a safeguard to prevent accidentally deleting an image. After the Image Delete option is chosen, a screen prompts Yes or No for deletion, with No being the default function.

THE VANISHING FRAME OF THE 35MM FORMAT

Currently, newer digital cameras are being developed with improved LCD and metering systems. At the same time, a break with the traditional 35mm format is being investigated.

Other avenues that have been explored in relation to digital photographic capture include a 360-degree camera that can provide the entire scene of an event, a different way of visual reporting. More information will be provided to the reader/viewer than in the standard "framed" image. Columbia University's Center for New Media began using this technology in the late 1990s.

Similar to what can be captured in a 360-degree camera, software programs can be used to patch together photographs taken at specified points using a tripod. The resulting image is a panoramic vision. The virtual reality process overlays JPEG photographic files to create one long image. Color corrections must be made to each individual image file for all images to match in regard to color adjustments and color balancing. When using this method for a 360-degree virtual reality, attention should be paid to the angle in which the images are shot so that the images can be stitched together accurately. After the images are stitched together, the entire long file is put in QuickTime format.

360 DEGREES

By John Pavlik, Ph.D., Professor and Executive Director of the Center for New Media, The Graduate School of Journalism, Columbia University

Photojournalists have always worked within the constraints of existing photographic technology. Most fundamentally, the traditional camera places a frame around the field of view, typically permitting the photojournalist to record a roughly 105-degree field of view at most, using a super-wide-angle lens. Digital imaging systems that have been developed since the mid-1990s permit photojournalists to expand their photographic field of view to an entire 360-degree field of view and yet maintain the photographic frame to focus attention.

One system (www.remotereality.com) uses standard digital still or video cameras attached to a special lens and parabolic mirror system. Using such a 360-degree camera, the photojournalist can capture through a single photograph an entire scene, such as a street protest, political convention, or crime scene. The 360-degree image can be placed on the web, and viewers can navigate the entire scene by mouse or keyboard control. The journalist has a variety of image presentation options and can select the initial 105-degree view that is now familiar to most and then automatically pan, tilt, or zoom around the entire 360-degree view or permit the audience member to explore the 360-degree image or video.

Applications of 360-degree imaging are wide reaching. Although most news organizations that have to date experimented with 360-degree imaging have used it in feature stories, APBnews.com and students at Columbia University's Center for New Media used a 360-degree camera to photograph the location where four New York City police officers shot Amadou Diallo in a sensational case in February 1999 (see Figure 3.6).

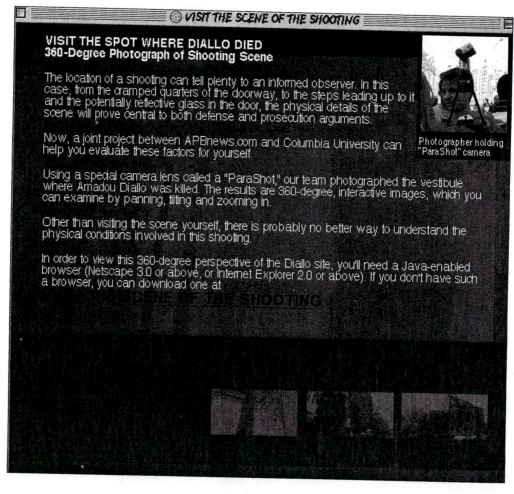

FIGURE 3.6

Joint Project Using a 360-Degree Camera

New APB News, Inc. and Columbia University.

THE BULLET-POCKED HALLWAY WHERE DIALLO DIED

zoom

Description: Dozens of bullet holes line the sheet-rock walls inside the vestibule where Amadou Diallo was fatally shot 19 times. Most are labeled in black marker by investigators. The other writings are poems and letters dedicated to the slain immigrant.

In the Forums: What can you learn from the physical evidence in the hallway? Was racism or a tragic mistake most responsible for the Diallo shooting?

INSTRUCTIONS: CLICK AND DRAG TO LOOK AROUND. PRESS 'A' TO ZOOM IN OR 'Z' TO ZOOM OUT. CLICK ON A RED BULLSEYE TO CHANGE YOUR POINT OF VIEW.

Choose a view ↕

Content generated by ParaShot(TM) Web System. CycloVision Technologies, Inc. http://www.cyclovision.com/

FIGURE 3.7

Panoramic View Shot with a 360-Degree Camera

New APB News, Inc. and Columbia University.

Viewers can go online and see the vestibule where Diallo was standing when he was shot, panning, tilting, or zooming in or out anywhere in the doorway, and examining the bullet holes and inscriptions written inside the apartment entryway. Clicking on the doorway opens a 360-degree view outside Diallo's apartment, permitting viewers to examine the street where Diallo lived and see his apartment building in the wider context of the neighborhood (see Figure 3.7).

Other emerging imaging technologies, such as dynamic range cameras, which expose each pixel in an image differently or dynamically, are poised to further transform photojournalism. Existing photographic technology, analogue or digital, has limited latitude to simultaneously render bright and dark portions of a scene.

Imagine photographing from indoors a window bathed in sunlight. If the bright scene outside were properly exposed, the interior of the room would appear to be in very deep shadow or almost all black. On the other hand, if you exposed properly for the interior, the outside scene would be bleached almost all white. This problem can be solved by using a dynamic range camera developed by Professor Shree Nayar (see http://www.cs.columbia.edu/CAVE/). Each pixel is exposed differentially, so dark areas of a scene can be highly exposed and bright areas can be underexposed. A scene of both bright and dark areas can now be captured in one recording.

AREAS FOR DISCUSSION

- Compare the theoretical digital chain to traditional prepress preparation of photographs. Has anything been lost? Has anything been gained?

- Compare and contrast the different ways in which light is recorded on film and on CCDs.

- Research early additive color photography processes in comparison to the RGB color filter coating or grid used in digital cameras to render color images.

- Predict what changes will occur within visual reporting as technology evolves to accommodate the possibility of higher-quality images for web publishing.

chapter 4

SCANNING AND PREPRESS TOOLS FOR WEB PUBLICATIONS

When preparing scanned images for web publication, file formats and resolution are different from those used for traditional print publication. The images will be viewed as screen images only. Therefore, these images will remain low-resolution images. As discussed in Chapter 1, the primary file formats for images published in online publications are JPEG or GIF. Some web-authoring software programs favor one over the other. These two file formats are cross-platform and have become industry standards. However, different forms of image compression are used. PNG is a file format that is available with some software for web image files. This file format requires a plug-in for some web browsers.

IMAGE COMPRESSION AND FILE FORMATS

Image compression relies on the fact that some digital data is expendable because the absence of some of the visual information will not be detected by the naked eye. The three basic types of image compression methods are lossless (in which no information is lost during the compression and decompression process), lossy (in which some information is lost during the process), and visually lossless (the process used by Photo CD in which data is sorted as important or unimportant and the unimportant data is deleted).

The JPEG (Joint Photographic Experts Group) file format is a lossy compression file format designed specifically for photographic images, supporting 24-bit color (millions of colors). The quality of the image compression is set on a sliding scale from low to medium to high. JPEG compressions work by averaging areas of similar color. Therefore, the higher the amount of compression, the more averaging that takes place. A medium setting with baseline optimized selected under format options renders an image quality "good enough" for web publication. Selecting progressive under format options lets the JPEG image gradually download as the web page is being viewed. However, this requires more RAM from the viewer's computer (see Figure 4.1).

GIF or CompuServ GIF (Graphic Interchange Format) uses lossless LZW compression, which is most effective with images that have large areas of continuous color and images with fine detail and/or type. The GIF format can handle only 8-bit images (256 colors), which can cause dithering of photographic images. However, monitors that are the least common denominator in viewing are limited to 256 colors. The GIF has two types: 87a, in which all pixels are opaque, and 89a, in which some pixels can be made transparent to let portions of the web page show through.

When saving an image in the GIF file format in Photoshop, first convert the image to indexed color mode by going to the Image menu, selecting Mode, and then selecting Indexed Color. The GIF color palette box will open (see Figure 4.2).

Four specifications can be set: Palette, Color Depth, Colors, and Dither. The palette choices are Exact, System (Macintosh), System (Windows), Web, Uniform, and Adaptive. The Exact palette will be available if the image has 256 colors or fewer. In this option, Photoshop will build an RGB color palette for the image. The Macintosh and Windows options are both 8-bit color tables but

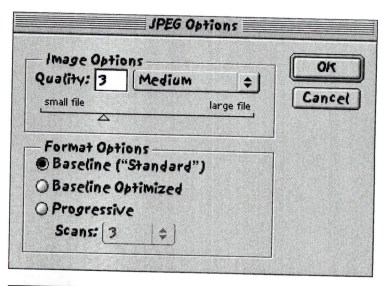

FIGURE 4.1

JPEG Options

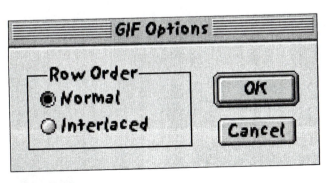

Indexed Color dialog box showing:
Palette: Web
Color Depth: Other
Colors: 216
Options — Dither: None
Color Matching: ● Faster ○ Best
□ Preserve Exact Colors
OK, Cancel, ☑ Preview

FIGURE 4.2

Indexed Color

limit the way in which the image will appear on either platform. The Web palette will render 8-bit color used by most web browsers and is the best choice when using Index Color mode images. The Adaptive palette choice will cause Photoshop to build a color table that includes only the most common colors in the image.

The Color Depths option will adjust depending on which palette is selected. The highest bit depth, 8, is the best selection if it is not automatically set. The Colors menu should be set at 256 if the bit depth is 8. If the Dither option is selected, Photoshop will simulate any colors of the Indexed Color Image that do not exist in the color table. This option is available only for Macintosh. It is preferable to set the Dither option to None. However, if the Exact color palette has been selected, dithering will not occur.

The GIF Options box will appear with two display options for Row Order (see Figure 4.3). The Normal option renders the image on the screen in lines appearing from top to bottom. The Interlaced option renders the image rapidly by using oversized pixels until the color area is filled with normal pixel size and resolution.

As was mentioned above, when part of an image is needed for a web page (similar to a cutout on a newspaper page), the image should be saved as a GIF89 file to ensure that the other pixels are transparent.

GIF Options dialog box showing:
Row Order
● Normal
○ Interlaced
OK, Cancel

FIGURE 4.3

GIF Options

To save an image as a GIF89 file, first make sure the version of Photoshop you are using contains the export filter. Go to the File menu and select Export; GIF89 should be listed. If not, it can be downloaded from the Adobe web site and dropped into the Import/Export folder in the Photoshop Plug-ins folder.

Creating a Transparent Background with GIF89

To create a transparent background with GIF89, follow this procedure:

1. Select the part of the RGB image that will appear on the web page using one of the selection tools. For best results, use the lasso tool or create a clipping path with the pen tool and change it into a selection (described in Chapter 10).

2. Copy the selection.

3. Paste the selection into a new layer, making sure the Preserve Transparency box is checked on the layer option tab (see Figure 4.4).

4. Turn off the background layer, and keep the transparent layer active (see Figure 4.4).

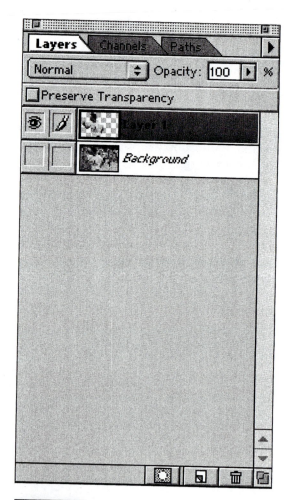

FIGURE 4.4

Background Layer and Selection Layer

Photo by Vernon Bryant.

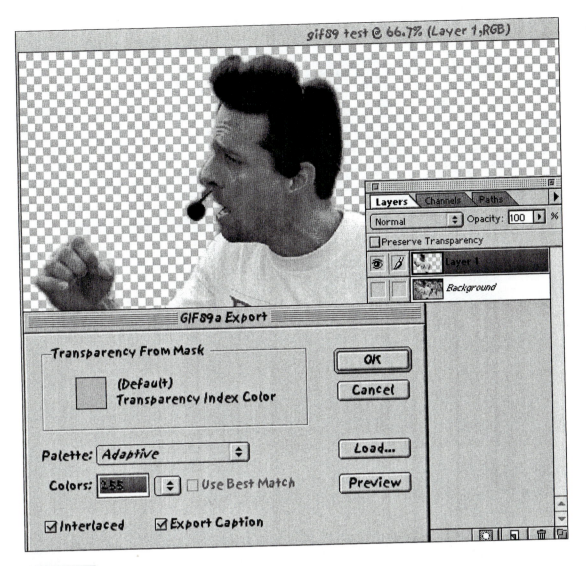

FIGURE 4.5

GIF Export Box

Note the transparency index color window.

Photo by Vernon Bryant.

5. Go to the File menu, select Export, and then select GIF89 (see Figure 4.5).

6. If the Transparency from Mask default is not desired, click on the box and set the desired color

7. In the Palette selection, choose from Exact, Adaptive, or System. If the Exact palette option is available, this provides the best image. It will be available only if the image has 256 or fewer colors. If the Exact palette choice is not available, choose Adaptive. The System choice uses 256 standard colors for either the Macintosh or Windows built-in color palette, which may produce unpredictable results.

8. Click the Preview button to see the image as it will appear on the web (see Figure 4.6).

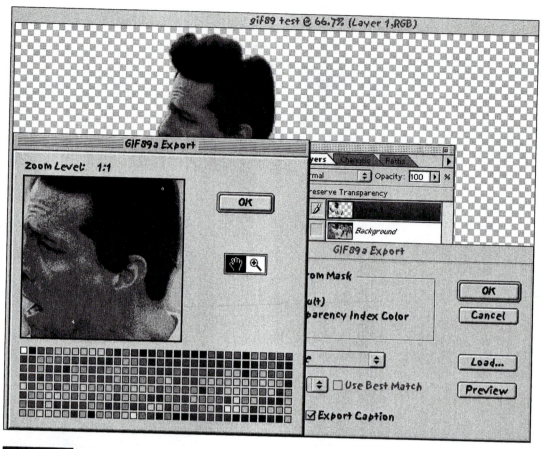

Palette of Colors and How the Selection Will Appear on the Web

Photo by Vernon Bryant.

9. If a caption accompanies the image, check the Export Caption box.
10. Click OK, and the Save box will appear, automatically adding the .gif extension on the file name. Make sure the name has eight or fewer characters.

PNG (Portable Network Graphic) is a newer graphic file format than JPEG or GIF. This file format compresses solid-color images and preserves details. This file format is available in Photoshop 6 and might require a plug-in to be viewed with a web browser.

COLOR CORRECTION FOR THE WEB

Because all images on the web are low-resolution images, there is no ideal image. Also, viewers' monitor calibration and whether more than 256 colors can be produced are not known and cannot be controlled. Images should always be prepared with the lowest common denominator of viewing in mind: a monitor 640 × 480 pixels with the capacity to view 256 colors. To color correct images for the web, change the monitor being used to 256 colors.

In addition to low resolution dictated by the medium, other factors that need to be considered are mode and size. As was stated in Chapter 1, images viewed on the web should be saved and color corrected in RGB mode (for

D-FW Weather: Currently -- TEMP 85° - WFAA Doppler radar

MAIN SECTIONS

To Subscribe

D-FW Metro

Texas & Southwest

Nation | World

Politics

Sports Day

Business

Entertainment

GuideLive

Today | Lifestyles

Travel

Weather

Opinion

Archives

Classifieds

Community

Contact us

Sponsor spotlight

What's on sale this Week at

Dallas schools lag further on TAAS

Dallas public schools fell slightly further behind state averages on the exam this year. That could almost triple the number of campuses deemed low-performing.
- Suburbs improve on test
- Results by district

Arena tower planned

The 30-story skyscraper in the Victory complex will house investor Tom Hicks' company and the offices of his sports teams

DNA tests rejected for condemned man

The top Texas criminal court said no to a judge's call for delaying Thursday's execution and allowing the retesting.

Area HMOs trim losses
- Rates expected to jump

BATTLE FOR THE CUP

Devils 7, Stars 3

Goalie Ed Belfour has led the Stars all through the playoffs, but he was not prepared for what hit him – and the Stars – last night in Game 1 of the Stanley Cup Finals.
- Photos
- Stars snap on Devils' night
- Green-gold fever takes hold of Dallas
- Cowlishaw: Road loss hits home
- More Cup coverage

New! Game 1 wallpaper of Belfour
800x600 | **1024x768** | **1280x1024**

Audio
(Requires free RealPlayer 7)
- Hitchcock: Devils too quick
- Belfour: Making bad decisions

Interactive
- Grade the Stars' Game 1 performance

FIGURE 4.7

The Dallasnews.com Home Page

Dallasnews.com, The *Dallas Morning News.*

JPEG) or indexed mode (for GIF). Size, as listed below, may be dictated by the publication layout template (see Figure 4.7).

It is important to keep the image files small for ease of downloading. Although software is being developed and packaged to make image preparation for the web more automatic, for general purposes all that is needed to prepare a singular photographic image for online publication is Photoshop. However, there are various software applications that automate workflow and archiving. These are discussed briefly below and in more detail in Chapters 5 and 8.

As images are saved, it is important to name or title the image file with a .jpg or .gif extension and eight or fewer characters for the name. This will ensure that the files can be read on any platform. When importing image files into web authoring programs or when using HTML formatting, this also provides fast file format identification while building the web page.

ACCESSING IMAGES FOR WEB PUBLICATION

An industry standard workflow for newspapers that publish dually (traditional print and on the web) has emerged to handle the organization of images being shot by one staff of photographers (see Figure 4.8).

FACTORS TO TAKE INTO CONSIDERATION
WHEN PREPARING IMAGES FOR THE WEB

- The correct file size, file format (JPEG or GIF), and resolution (72 for a Mac screen, 96 for a PC). Most online newspapers have standard sizes, for example, 200 pixels wide for thumbnail previews and 400 pixels wide for the larger image to which it is linked.

- Image mode: RGB (for JPEG) or Indexed (for GIF). These formats are for color or black and white images.

- Image cropping for screen viewing

- Image size for screen viewing

- Watermark of encryption (discussed in Chapter 11)

- Image as page entry for online viewing (discussed in Chapter 5)

- Choice of black and white or color images for online viewing

---

FIGURE 4.8

Preparing Images for the Web

At this time, few newspapers have a separate shooting staff for the web publication. Therefore, both publishing formats must pull from the same image database. Various software programs are on the market to handle this workflow (see the book website for updated information.)

Software applications such as Media Grid display thumbnails and files, allowing searches to be performed on different servers and libraries (libraries and archiving are discussed in Chapter 8). By using software applications to handle the workflow, attributes such as captions and bylines can be searched when pulling from image databases for web publishing. For example, if an image of a particular person needs to be pulled from the image database for the web publication, all of the images can be searched by name instead of having to open each and every one. Picture files can be added, deleted, or changed automatically, streamlining access for both publishing formats.

IMAGE CROPPING FOR WEB PUBLICATIONS

Surveys of photo directors of web publications reveal that most newspapers that publish dually do not have written guidelines addressing the recropping of images for the web when they are used in both publications. These surveys also reveal that many web photo editors recrop images to enhance the figure–ground relationship in the smaller view of the image. The relationship between the foreground and background of the image becomes more critical in a small image. The figure, or the main subject and focal point, of the image needs to fill a certain percentage of the frame so that what the photograph is about will be apparent to the viewer when it is viewed as a small image (see Figure 4.9).

FIGURE 4.9

East Timor Gunman

Agence Presse France.

However, each publication should set guidelines to ensure that if images are recropped, minimal areas of the parameter of the image frame are eliminated and no content is omitted (see Figures 4.10 and 4.11).

As is discussed in more detail in Chapter 2, the solution to handling small images on the web will evolve to be employing different concerns during the photo-editing process instead of recropping the image.

FIGURE 4.10

A Slightly Tighter Crop

This crop does not eliminate content but enhances the figure–ground relationship.

Agence Presse France.

FIGURE 4.11

After the Tighter Crop Is Applied

Agence Presse France.

Areas for Discussion

■ Discuss types of images that might or might not work well when viewed on the web.

■ Discuss ethical concerns of recropping images for the web when the image is published both in the traditional print format and in the web publication (see also Chapter 11).

chapter 5

PHOTO EDITING FOR WEB PUBLICATIONS AND THE ROLE OF ONLINE PHOTOJOURNALISM

PHOTO EDITING: TELLING A VISUAL STORY ONLINE

The basic principles of photo editing are the same for both mediums—traditional print and online publishing. The primary consideration is selecting storytelling photographs that can convey the fullest, most accurate sense of the situation being photographed. Such photographs must engage the heart and mind of the viewer while also expressing the most clear, compelling version of a truth that resulted from the act of bearing witness. This is at the heart of all photojournalism.

No photograph can tell the complete truth, and no photographer can be true witness to the totality of an event, situation, or human life. However, done well, photojournalism can bear witness to partial truths that convey both a highly specific moment in time as well as the undercurrents of larger truths about the human condition.

THE EVOLVING PROCESS OF NEW MEDIA PHOTO EDITING: PRINT VERSUS ONLINE

As a standard rule, many print newspaper projects that purport to be photo stories are in reality illustrated texts, in which each photo in the group corresponds to an event in the text. No real narrative thread is created by the photographs, and there is no real sequencing that might be visually driven. Changes in this formula should be made to better the evolution of the process of storytelling via the web (see Figure 5.1). What is needed are multiple points of view that create strong ties between individual photographs (see Figures 5.2 and 5.3).

from the Photo Desk

Figure 5.1 ■ Figure 5.2 ■ Figure 5.3

Examples of storytelling on the web showing visually driven sequencing.

FIGURE 5.1

Camera Works, Washingtonpost.com.

FIGURE 5.2

Camera Works,
Washingtonpost.com

FIGURE 5.3

Camera Works,
Washingtonpost.com

The shortcomings of the standard formula that has historically been used in print may stem more from the traditional process of story creation than from the inherent limitations of the print format, which include the restriction of space. Also, the shortcomings may stem from the age-old bias in print of text being deemed more important as a storytelling device than the visual image. The usual workflow in most news organizations in regard to print involves a planning process that offers more time and flexibility to reporters than photographers, and this compounds this bias.

Because the computer is a less ideal vehicle than traditional print for reading extended text, the same biases that thwart development of a visual narrative based on photojournalism in print are currently less apparent in the web environment. However, given the parentage of most web sites, it is clear that the institutional biases do carry over into the web environment. As newspaper web sites continue to evolve, there will be an ongoing and spirited conversation between editorial types, designers, and photo editors.

TIME, SPACE, AND THE USE OF TECHNOLOGY

Differences in Time

The discovery phases of the story are comparable in both mediums, but the web requires more constant communication as circumstances change or new inputs are added. Also, in print, on a big project, photographers and writers may toil for months until something is exactly right. On the web, it is more typical to be working backward from a known deadline that is ironclad. *Time* is the crucial variable on the web.

Thus, a primary difference that exists between editing photos for the web and editing for the print newspaper page is the speed of decision making required to work in the web news environment. Deadlines come in matters of minutes, if not seconds. Clear decisions about photographs must be made using the same values that govern the appearance of photos in print. To edit in the web environment and meet the deadline pressure, one must be very focused and very engaged in tracking the news of the moment while also being aware of past developments that are germane.

For print, there may be one deadline per day or tiered deadlines for additions/sections. For the web, a general rule of thumb is that the photograph is needed *before* it's shot. All content is needed immediately, and this applies to stories as well as photographs.

During this fast-paced photo-editing and decision-making process, one must operate from strong wellsprings of ethical judgment and a philosophical base for the use of photojournalism. Moral responsibility demands that one consider the implications of the photograph and its relationship to both subject and end viewer, but in web publishing, unlike print publishing, these decisions must play out in very tight time frames.

A strong daily awareness of news developments must be tied to past experiences as a photo editor. Over time, notwithstanding time pressures, a strong photo editor should be able to be decisive in weighing all the factors that might apply to a given situation. Yet at the same time, the photo editor can't operate by falling back on rote, familiar solutions to a specific circumstance. Each judgment call has to be weighed on its own calculus.

Differences in Space

How Many Photos Tell the Story?   In contrast to the fight for space between stories, ads, and photographs in traditional print, the amount of space is not a problem on the web. Because of the amount of "actual space" on the web in relation to the traditional print format, photos that didn't run because of space constraints can run on the web. This mindset of almost unlimited space complicates the photo-editing process by the very notion that more may be used than in print. As was mentioned above, the main focus should remain on visually narrative storytelling even when quantity of selection is not a limiting factor. (Media options are discussed in the next section.)

Differences in Size and the Importance of Good Cropping.   Because photographs in web publications tend to be smaller in size than those in print, the skill of cropping becomes very important. Optimal cropping becomes a major factor in making the most of the figure–ground relationship within the image frame (see Figure 5.4).

It is crucial that a photo editor be able to recognize the essential elements in every photograph and crop the space to highlight the main content. Lazy cropping or extensive use of highly complicated images does not work in the web environment. However, publishing a group of photographs that combines

SPECIAL SECTION: *The News-Sentinel presents this report to share the vision, dedication and self-sacrifice of the students with their community.*

Faith, antibiotics & good intentions

On a medical mission trip to Haiti, a group of Huntington College students put their faith and belief in humanity to the test.

Photos by ELLIE BOGUE
Story by ASHRAF KHALIL of The News-Sentinel

They were so few, and they came to a land that needs so much -- bearing little more than faith, antibiotics and good intentions.

"Sometimes I think, 'How dare we come down here for three weeks and think we're going to fix these people,' " said Heidi Martz, one of the 21 Huntington College students who traveled to Haiti in January for 20 days of medical clinics and soul-searching.

Huntington physician Dr. Bill Webb, who has been to Haiti more than 10 times in the past 14 years, led the students on their journey.

"He who dwells in the shelter of the Most High ... will say to the Lord, 'My refuge and my fortress.'" -- Psalms 91:1-2

FIGURE 5.4

Tightly cropped photograph with a large figure–ground relationship.

Fort Wayne News-Sentinel.

a complicated image with a more simplified image can be done successfully. This is presenting a visual story that moves from the general to the specific (see Figures 5.5 and 5.6). As computer display technology advances to incorporate high-definition television viewing standards, this situation might change and a different kind of aesthetic language could become successful on the web.

from the Photo Desk

Figure 5.5 ■ Figure 5.6

Differences in the figure–ground relationship of images published as a series on the web. Figure 5.5 is a visually layered image and Figure 5.6 is a simplified, tightly cropped image.

No longer strangers in a strange land

Story by LISA KIM BACH, Photos by ELLIE BOGUE *of The News@Sentinel*

Memories of the day Saigon fell play across Long Tran's face like a flickering piece of movie video.

On April 30, 1975, while the Viet Cong celebrated victory in Vietnam, Tran was arrested, herded onto a truck and shipped to the countryside. For the next $5^1/_2$ years, he would pay the price of being an officer in the enemy army -- Imprisonment in a re-education camp, where rehabilitation meant forced labor and a meager bowl of salted rice each day.

FIGURE 5.5

Visually Layered Image

Fort Wayne News-Sentinel.

The night the family Tran family arrives at the airport. Via looks around bewildered and tired after a long day of travel.

Ellie Bogue
Staff Photographer
Photographed June 18, 1996

Fort Wayne , IN USA

Return to story

FIGURE 5.6

Tightly Cropped Image

Fort Wayne News-Sentinel.

A 1999 study by the Poynter Institute looking at newspapers that publish dually—online and in traditional print—found that photo editors of the online version were routinely recropping images for the online publication. Many newspapers have created written guidelines concerning this issue. The most important factor to consider if recropping is allowed is not to lose content.

However, no matter whether the image is to be published on the web or in print, a bad crop is still a bad crop. In the perfect world, the crop would be the same for publishing formats. As was stated above, as a different kind of aesthetic language develops, what might change is the choice of images used for each. It the image has too much detail to be shown small on the web, cropping it might not be the right action to take. The right action might be picking a different image that will hold up better when displayed small.

Another difference inherent in photographs published online is resolution. Photographs that are published online are low-resolution images in either JPEG or GIF format, so there are different concerns than in producing a high-resolution CMYK image for print. Therefore, the skill of color balancing to arrive at maximum image fidelity for web publishing also becomes important. (Color balancing for the web is covered in Chapter 4.)

Differences in the Technology

File Size. Although space is not a problem, bandwidth might be. In other words, the online publication can use as many photos as necessary, but file size must be taken into consideration. Most viewers/readers will not wait for a large image file to download. Although computers have had high-definition television viewing standards for a number of years, the problem on the web is twofold:

1. Most computers do not run at this high resolution, so the lowest common denominator for screen resolution is used.

2. Because of bandwidth concerns and file size, sites have to be built to be accessed by a slow modem.

As technology evolves and more viewers access the web via cable, satellite, DSL, or T1 lines, sites on the web and the images displayed on them will improve.

The Process and Technology: Planning and Media Options. Technology becomes an issue for many news organizations' sites in establishing how to handle photos on a daily basis. This greatly affects the decision of whether to run many photographs or none at all.

In addition to the element of time affecting the planning process, the inherent bells and whistles of online technology have a profound effect. The web requires full collaboration from the outset because of the complexities of the tools to publish online for multiple user platforms.

The planning process begins and ends with a group meeting of photographer, photo editor, text editor, designer, and production person (coder). All must come to a consensus about the main elements of the story and how various kinds of media are going to be used to tell the story. This is considerably different from print, in which typically two or three people are involved until the very end. Because of multiple media options to tell the story, the complexity of developing a strong narrative structure is greatly increased. The process is much closer to making a movie than producing a classic print photo story (see Figure 5.7).

ONLINE	TRADITIONAL PRINT
■ Define story content and audience	■ Define story content and audience
■ Plan visual strategy/budget	■ Plan visual strategy/budget
■ Identify best multimedia formats for storytelling coverage	■ Assign appropriate photojournalists to cover story
■ Execute coverage	■ Execute coverage
■ Organize and edit all media formats	■ Edit photographs
■ Prepare visuals/text within web authoring application	■ Page editor constructs print package
■ Edit text and visuals for accuracy and storytelling strengths	
■ Post visual package online	

FIGURE 5.7

The Visual Communication Planning/Editing Process

Ironically, while the speed of the medium imposes certain pressures, so too does the range of technical possibilities available to shape content packages. Unlike print, the web affords a photo editor the chance to mix media with a resulting range of display possibilities for every story. In contrast, print generally offers at best the chance to provide a grouping of images on a page, accompanied by story text and brief captions.

On the web a photo editor has to be cognizant of the opportunities afforded by mixing still photos with video, audio, and text. Because of this the process is more complicated than in print. A photo editor has to know more about the ways in which these media communicate independently and together to make strong narrative stories.

The sheer variety of browsers, connection speeds, display devices, and hardware and software platforms makes arriving at the broadest possible solution extremely challenging. Knowledge of computer technology and of the best ways to arrive at technical solutions to presenting content is crucial for success. One must be able to use the technical knowledge to judge the merits of content presentation and image quality throughout the production process.

At the same time we have so many other formats we can choose from, such as a slideshow Flash (see Figure 5.8).

FIGURE 5.8

Storytelling on the Web

The players:	Photographer
	Photo editor
	Text editor
	Designer
	Online production person (coder)
Media options:	Still photographs
	QuickTime VR panorama 360° camera coverage
	Video
	Audio
	Written story

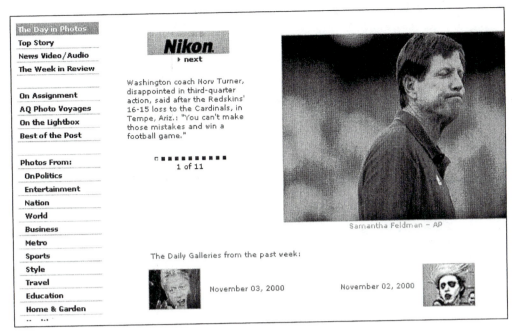

FIGURE 5.9

Use of Thumbnails

Small thumbnails can be used as links in addition to larger photographs on a web page.

Washingtonpost.com.

Navigation.   An important part of the visual narrative involved in web story-telling is the navigation of the web page. Photographs can be used to link to another story on another page, to larger galleries of photos, or to a larger view of the selected image (see Figures 5.9 and 5.10).

There is still much that will be done in experimentation with navigation and the linking of content in visual presentations. As Tom Kennedy, Director of Photography and Design at washingtonpost.com, explains, "Repeated, simple,

FIGURE 5.10

Camera Works' On the Lightbox

This feature allows the viewer/reader to drag an image onto the web site light box to see a larger view of the image.

Washingtonpost.com.

- Hierarchy of size of photos

- Variation of size and proportion

- Repetition of size and proportion

- Combining stills and video

- Audio in addition to text captioning (captions on steroids—Brian Storm)

- The relationship of background color with photographs

- Text on photographs

- Using graphics and photographs

- Page navigation

FIGURE 5.11

Elements to Consider in Photo-Driven Web Page Design

consistent navigation is essential to building a mass audience. That said, the rules of good web design are still very much in flux." The navigation of the site is part of the design (or form) of the web page and is part of the function (see Figure 5.11).

Web Page Design and the Dominant Element. Notwithstanding the recent Eye-track study sponsored by the Poynter Institute and Stanford (www.poynter.org) and the function of navigation as mentioned above, the basis of good layout on the web still remains a matter of playing strong photos against the backdrop of a simple page design.

In many respects, as in print publishing, use of photos in this way can serve to attract viewers. In many respects, web design resembles the task confronting a magazine cover designer trying to make his or her product stand out from the clutter of newsstand racks. How does strong photography make it more possible to attract attention and communicate from a very cluttered landscape? Tom Kennedy says, "I don't think there is one right answer, but it must be at the heart of every design decision."

Recent studies show that unlike traditional print pages, web images have very little impact on the viewing audience. These studies go as far as saying that users go to the story first and then sometimes go back and look at the images.

Although most online publications have standard design layout templates for pages within the web site (similar to standard page design of traditional print publications), the concept of the photographic image as an entry to the page should not be abandoned yet. Other studies point out the small size of photographic images on the web as being a primary factor of lack of interest in viewing. Another study looking at the use of photographs and design of three U.S. newspapers publishing online found that most photographs run about 3.5 × 2.5 inches and that this may be a factor that contributes to text being the dominant online newspaper content. Also affecting image viewing online is the fact that because the web is not like a broadsheet, the photographs cannot all be seen at the same time.

THE REPURPOSING (REUSE) ISSUE

Because of the differences mentioned previously in this chapter dealing with space, time, and technology, the decision of whether to run the same images online as in the traditional print format may vary for many reasons. Tom Kennedy states,

> We view one of our primary missions as presenting the photography done by print *Post* staff photographers as fully as possible. We have the opportunity to regularly run more photos than those used by the newspaper, and tell a more complete story as a result. We often run the same photos as those that appear in the newspaper on a given topic. However, differences mentioned earlier cause us to make different choices on the same story as well. In my opinion, the photo editing on the *Post* web site tends to be slightly edgier and its presentation more dramatic than that of the newspaper.

THE ROLE OF PHOTOJOURNALISM ON THE WEB

By Keith Hitchens, Director of Photography, Fort Wayne News-Sentinel

Like traditional print products, how photos fit into the design affects the overall relationship between text and image. However, there is a different set of rules for web pages than for the print product. There has to be. An example is QuickTime Virtual Reality. This method of visual storytelling cannot be done in traditional print.

Also, the high interest in web publishing involving the use of video and audio is spurring the evolution of the method of online visual storytelling. The main outlet for these new media publishing formats and the inherent new tools is the web.

However, the basic role of photojournalism is the same, even though photographs are viewed in a different medium and consequently are not seen or perceived in the same way. As in traditional print, the photographs have to be able to communicate visually alone, without a story attached. At this time, photojournalism is one of the most underused media on the web.

THE EVOLUTION OF PHOTOJOURNALISM ON THE WEB

By Tom Kennedy, Director of Photography and Design, washingtonpost.com

I think there is a strong likelihood of a different evolutionary path for the role of online photojournalism in contrast to what has come to be in traditional print. The web photojournalist has to be aware of the implications of more media being mixed than one working solely in print. To be successful, the photo editor will have to know how to work collaboratively with people who are highly skilled in other editing disciplines yet retain an overall sense of the value of using photojournalism to communicate information.

In many respects, the true value of photojournalism as a communications medium may be more revealed on the web because it can be blended seamlessly with inputs of video, audio, and text. Each medium can do what it does best while working to create a whole greater than the sum of the parts.

On the web, we have the time to develop long-form, narrative photojournalism. The great essays of *Life* photographers Gene Smith and Leonard McComb present an excellent paradigm for what can be done on the web. In addition, other elements can add information and texture that will appeal to all the senses of the end user. Unlike print, in which space constraints often dictate the selection of photos, the web offers a chance to create longer narrative projects that can convey more sides of the story. Complexity, nuance, ambiguity, irony, and depth can all be expressed as part of the narrative voice. The plethora of choices will inevitably affect the vision of both photographer and photo editor.

Another aspect of the web is that it allows for the creation of an ongoing dialogue between subject, photographer, and end user in ways that cannot occur in print because of space limitations and the lack of a capacity to build interactivity. Message boards tied to stories allow end users to question subjects and photographers alike. The recorded conversations with subjects in the field can be used as part of a story, and the photographer's observations can be recorded afterward to clarify why he or she chose to document the events in that way. These complexities in the communications process actually enable us to tell a more complete story, but they will require us to be more sophisticated in our methods of presentation.

Print publications are now largely the province of the controlled and contrived image. "Approximations of reality" based on a complete, willing collusion between subject and photographer drive out documentary photography and photojournalism. The photographer's individual imagination and manipulativeness have come to mean much more than skill in relating to a subject and drawing him or her out through a delicately choreographed ballet of developing mutual trust that is more characteristic of pure photojournalism. This is a direct result of the emergence of our celebrity culture coupled with the economics of print publishing that preclude support for lengthy assignments. Today, having five days on a print assignment is a luxury.

In the near future, web photojournalists will work side by side with counterparts who choose to remain in the world of print. The former will be required to know more image capture platforms initially and be more familiar with the impact of audio and video. Over time, though, technology may lead us back to a single-system camera that is capable of recording images with sufficient fidelity to satisfy both print and web requirements.

Also, web photo editors and photographers will need to be able to develop longer form narrative stories rather than trying to reduce all experience to a single strong photograph. I think the roles are comparable.

Still photographs, whether singly or in groups, can tell powerful stories about the human condition while also providing crucial information. The early photos from Kosovo and the more recent photos showing the cruelty perpetrated on innocent civilians in Sierra Leone are two examples. In both cases, photographs stirred human emotions on many continents, and the response of citizens helped to give politicians the moral courage to act.

Because the web world is still in its infancy, it is unclear whether video will ever fully supplant still photography there as it has on television. I hope that both will coexist so that a richer type of storytelling can be developed.

Certain web sites clearly mimic contemporary print products by using single images as visual headlines to attract viewers. This is a very limited use of the medium, but it is easy and safe and helps to curtail the costs of production.

Nonetheless, I think the smartest web sites are discovering the power of the photo essay translated into this new medium. When strong still photographs are sequenced to build a strong story line and then coupled with powerful audio and video, the storytelling power that is unleashed is really amazing. Brian Storm of MSNBC coined the term *captions on steroids* when referring to audio coupled with still photography published on the web. Much of our effort is currently going into using new software and hardware to unify disparate media elements into a seamless story presentation.

Meanwhile, newspapers continue to show strong individual photojournalism images every day. Yet too often, these are the exception—pure nuggets surrounded by the fool's gold of emblematic and iconographic images that pretend to be comprehensive but really signify nothing. They are the products of limited imaginations, safe coverage plans, and underinvestment in the time necessary to connect with subjects to reveal significant facts about the human condition. They seem to be a new form of visual shorthand, reminding me of the cries of long-ago newsboys hawking papers by shouting headlines out from urban street corners.

In the end, if certain economic conditions don't come into reality, the constraints of time on the web may prove as pernicious as the limitations of space currently are in print.

I remain optimistic that the web's inherent opportunities for experimentation are today sowing the seeds of a new kind of visual storytelling. The rewards from such experimentation are already in evidence for photojournalists, photo editors, and viewers alike. Once exposed to these meaty projects, a certain percentage of the population will demand and support such expressions as part of the daily flow of storytelling content.

I liken today's period on the web to that time when nickelodeon images were giving way to the first silent feature films. The crudeness of the technology, lack of clear financial infrastructure, and other facts are comparable as an analogy. But the potent rewards are already causing a steady stream of experienced talent to the web, and the best students just out of college are making their way to the web with increasing frequency.

Job Skills

To work as a successful visual journalist for an online news publication or for news publications that publish dually—both in traditional print and online—a person must be a neo-Renaissance photojournalist. As is discussed in Chapter 6, a variety of talent and skills are needed to be a good photo editor in traditional print. However, translating this to the web environment compounds the job. Although many more specific skill sets are required, a comprehensive grounding in "good journalism" remains essential.

Possible Scenarios

The field of photojournalism will always be changing, and as was stated previously, advancements in technology do affect the industry. These changes might or might not be good for journalists or photojournalists—the content providers.

As this book goes to print, dot-com news publications are cutting back on journalists across the board. Many news businesses are laying off content people and hiring more employees in the field of advertising. This trend of downsizing content personnel is nationwide, and some news publications are just quitting publishing online all together.

Because most new front-end systems are now offering direct publishing to the web, this cookie cutter "site in a box" concept is spreading to more and more news sites. What this means to photography is that more and more sites are being published with predefined image use or a lack of image use altogether. And as the use of handheld devices to access news content increases, the need for photographs in this arena decreases.

On a positive note, as technology continues to advance, computer resolution and use of digital video may increase in online publishing. Therefore, image quality will be considerably improved. As photojournalists adapt to the changing industry and publishing formats—regardless of image size and resolution—content will always be the most important ingredient.

AREAS FOR DISCUSSION

- Define visual storytelling and discuss various ways in which this might be different when publishing on the web versus traditional print.
- Discuss reasons why a photo editor might choose another photograph for the web publication instead of running the same photograph that appeared in the traditional print publication.
- Discuss the element of time in relation to web publishing.

chapter 6

Photo Editing for Traditional Print Publications

Defining the Photo Editor

Photo editor is a relatively new position in most newsrooms. Photo editors were virtually nonexistent until the 1970s. The *Dallas Morning News* hired its first photo editor in 1979, and the *Boston Globe* waited until 1987.

Before the position of photo editor evolved, photo departments were managed by chief photographers whose main job was to order supplies, give out assignments, and make sure deadlines were met. They were expected to run the photography operation as a service department, not to edit film.

In the late 1960s and early 1970s, a few journalism schools such as the University of Missouri, Ohio University, Indiana University, and Western Kentucky University began to graduate photographers with an emphasis on the journalism in the word *photojournalism*. A few enlightened newspaper editors wanted their photography departments to be more than service departments, to broaden their contribution and be more proactive in the newsrooms, to become a desk of origin.

Although the concept was well intentioned, photo editors got off to a rather inauspicious beginning at many newspapers. More often than not, editors picked the best photographer on the staff and said, "You're a photo editor." What many editors failed to realize was that just because a person is a skilled photographer, it does not always follow that he or she will necessarily become a good photo editor. There are management, leadership, and organizational skills to be considered.

A good photo editor is a Renaissance person of sorts. A photo editor must be the following:

- An excellent journalist, first and foremost
- A communicator
- A reader advocate
- An assignment editor
- A film editor
- A motivator and supporter
- A critic, coach, and teacher
- An organizer and planner
- An originator of ideas
- A diplomat
- A protector of the photographer's vision

Maria Mann, Agence Presse France's director of photography for North America, says that what a photo editor must *not* be is a photographer who is simply tired of taking photos. Mann says a photo editor must have the following:

- A true passion for the art of editing and an absolute love of images and respect for those who create them
- The ability to seek out the details of big stories that might be subtler but that are essential to tying everything together or the ability to seek out the big details in small stories
- A hunger to know and, in turn, to show why global events are important and how they can affect almost everyone
- The good sense to feel as proud of successful coverage as the photographer who shot it and to rejoice in the photographer's work
- A strong gut instinct about what should and should not be shown
- A conviction and a willingness to accept responsibility for his or her actions, good or bad
- The courage to go against convention when the situation merits
- Above all, the ability to instill in others the passion and the need to learn

Mann says that to face these challenges, editors and photographers also need to be armed with the following:

- A strong desire to document and change the way things work in this world
- A strong sense of right and wrong
- A strong sense of news, not just the obvious, but the nose to "smell" a potentially good story and monitor the progression of events and gambling on committing resources
- Good powers of observation
- An affinity for local, domestic, and international news; knowledge of political science; and at least a rudimentary understanding of macroeconomics because they are all interconnected, always
- An ability to write a firsthand account from the scene

- A second language (It's not just the language; it's about culture, history, and people of not just one but many countries. Do not deny this wonderful gift. Do not confine yourself to our little American world, for knowledge of other languages and cultures can't help but contribute to your growth as a photographer or photo editor.)
- An unending curiosity

THE PLANNING PROCESS: BEGIN WITH THE PHOTO ASSIGNMENT AND PHOTO DESK OPERATION

Good photojournalism starts with the assignment or, to use the more proper term, the photo request. It is a request because not all assignments should or can be carried out. If the subject of the request is nonvisual, the photographer is already in trouble. If there is insufficient information, the photographer is in the dark as to the story direction. If the assignment load is too heavy, photographers can't go early and stay late, a key to producing good photographs.

Successful news photography, more than any other means of expression available to the newspaper, depends on a combination of commitment, organization, planning, teamwork, talent, and technology. If there is poor planning in any area, the images will fall short of their potential. The photo editor is at the very center of all this. When those factors don't come together to produce a good news photograph, here are some of the things a managing editor is likely to hear:

- From the photographer: "I didn't have the right information."
- From the photo assignment editor: "No one turned in an assignment."
- From the city editor: "Our reporter was on the spot. It wasn't my job to get the photographer there."
- From the writer: "I wrote my story. What else do you want me to do?"
- From the page designer: "The picture doesn't go with the story."
- From the reader: "I don't get it."

The last comment is the most critical one and the one for which there is no credible answer. We are always judged by what hits the reader's doorstep.

A good photo editor will try to get into the photo request process as soon as possible. Planning meetings are a good place to kill bad ideas, to come up with better ideas, and to find visual potential in stories that may have been overlooked by originating editors.

The *Dallas Morning News* has worked hard to refine its photo desk operation in the newsroom. The work has paid off; the photo staff has received four Pulitzer Prizes and four Robert F. Kennedy Awards for Photojournalism in the last 13 years.

Paula Nelson, Assistant Director of Photography at the *Dallas Morning News,* says that to influence the visual presentation, the photo editor must be involved in the planning process from the very beginning. When a photo editor is involved early the planning process—the point at which the story is really being formulated—the photo editor is better able to influence the direction of the assignment and even the storytelling. It is at this point that the photo editor can make suggestions, ask questions and gather information, all of which will lead to a better opportunity to tell the story visually.

Nelson says that armed with this information, the photo editor can start thinking about selecting a photographer whose talents are suited to the type

FIGURE 6.1

Working Together

The *Dallas Morning News* photo editor Anne Farrar discusses caption information with staff photographer Kim Ritzenthaler at the photo desk. Photo editors and photographers work closely together to ensure that the best images are published.

Photo by Andy Scott, The *Dallas Morning News*.

of story that will be told. Some photographers have technical strengths; some excel in composition, and some in basic creativity. Although a good photojournalist should be versatile, some excel in sports, some in portraiture, and others in news. If the photographer can be matched with the type of assignment in which she or he excels, the result will be a more cohesive and thoughtful project (see Figure 6.1).

Another important reason, Nelson says, for the photo editor to be represented in the planning process is to contribute visual thinking. The writer and the editor will present their view of the story and how they believe it will be told in words. The photo editor, thinking visually, can use his or her own creative process and experience as a photographer to present ways to capture the story in a visual form. It is also important to get the photographer involved as soon as possible. Because photography is subjective and no two people will approach a subject exactly the same way—vision is unique—photographers should be given the opportunity to put their own spin on ideas.

USING A VISUAL LANGUAGE

When performing their duties—whether it is talking to photographers about photo requests, during a film editing session, or talking with editors outside the photo department—photo editors should use the visual language. It should never just be "This is a great photograph, run it big" or "This image doesn't work."

The value of a photograph should always be discussed in visual terms: impact, information, layering, point of entry, dominant foreground, informational background, graphic quality, sense of place, mood, emotion, intimacy, juxtaposition, composition, and quality of light. When the visual language is promoted and taught in the newsroom, a culture is created in which people have a common understanding (not to be confused with agreement) and a better chance of collaboration and integration of words, photographs, and infographics, the three voices of the print medium (see Figures 6.2 through 6.9).

from the Photo Desk

Figure 6.2

There is a visual language that is used to discuss the value of an image. When the language is not used, it is hard to explain why a photograph is successful or not very good other than "I like it" or "It doesn't work for me." In the case of the Sudanese boy and his brother the use of juxtaposition advances the storytelling quality of the image. The photographer contrasted the starving children with the cattle behind them, animals that most of the world understands to be food. She was able to visually capture the irony of starving people who hold cattle sacred and therefore continue to suffer famine. This photograph is also an example of a dominant foreground and an informational background. The reader enters the image through the poignant starving children, and the eye moves on to the rest of the information—in this case, the cattle behind them.

FIGURE 6.2

Starvation in Sudan

Judy Walgren, The *Dallas Morning News*.

from the Photo Desk

Figure 6.3 ■ Figure 6.4 ■ Figure 6.5

These three photographs have a graphic quality that makes the images visually appealing. The converging lines in the hands and the feet of the ballet dancers create a strong point of entry into the image as well as making the photograph aesthetically pleasing. The point of entry is still the intense young face in spite of the strong graphics created by other tables and the hundreds of chess pieces waiting for players. Good photographers always try to make everyday situations visually interesting. The trick is to not use any one technique to the point of making it a cliché.

FIGURE 6.3

Converging Lines

Gayle Shomer, The *Charlotte Observer.*

FIGURE 6.4

Chess Tournament

Todd Sumlin, The *Charlotte Observer*.

FIGURE 6.5

Ballet Feet

Allison Smith, The *Dallas Morning News*.

FIGURE 6.6

Going for the Ball

William Snyder, The *Dallas Morning News*.

from the Photo Desk

Figure 6.6
Figure 6.7

The same visual language is used to place value on sports photography. It doesn't matter that there is only one player in the picture; all of the arms going for the basketball create a graphic appeal and an excellent image. A good sports photographer knows that all of the action is not limited to the field of play. By looking for the emotion in an event the photographer captured the women's Nigerian relay team's extreme joy of competing and winning in the Summer Olympics.

FIGURE 6.7

Olympic Glory

Ken Geiger, The *Dallas Morning News*.

It is the photojournalist's job to visually report on the human condition. If there is a common weakness in the visual report of most newspapers, it is the lack of humor. That is not to say that photographers should make humorous photographs out of serious situations, but there are funny things out in the world that happen every day. Just as there are tragedy and sadness in our daily lives, there is also humor, and it is part of the human condition. It is perfectly legitimate to give the reader a chuckle from time to time and still be considered a serious photographer.

Sometimes it is the photographer's job to generate an aesthetic appreciation for the subject. The quality of light created the mood of the moment as floodlights illuminated a church in Switzerland as night fell after a heavy storm.

FIGURE 6.8

Cherubs

David Leeson, The *Dallas Morning News.*

FIGURE 6.9

Nightfall

Arno Balzarini, Agence Presse France.

from the Photo Desk
Figure 6.10 ■ Figure 6.11

Photographs can be categorized as either active or passive images. Active photographs are images that show real people engaged in real events in real time. The photo of a policewoman having a showdown with a gun-wielding youth who was threatening to commit suicide on a city street is an active photograph. The portrait of a successful young couple outside of their mansion is a passive photograph. Passive photographs are those that show people in situations in which their central purpose is to have their photographs taken for the newspaper. Many times, photos are made long after an event transpired. This is where the passive image is a legitimate approach to an assignment, usually an environmental photograph.

FIGURE 6.10
Showdown (Active Image)
Allison Smith, The *Dallas Morning News*.

ACTIVE VERSUS PASSIVE PHOTOGRAPHS

A very simple way for photo editors to talk about news photography is to categorize images as either "active" or "passive." Active photographs are those that show real people engaged in real events in real time (see Figure 6.10). Passive photographs are those that show people in situations in which their essential purpose is to have their photograph taken for the newspaper (see Figure 6.11).

Obviously, the preference is for active photography because it brings the insight of documentary photojournalism to the daily mix of the newspaper. It allows photographers to produce images that tell readers about their community and the world in a way that informs, inspires, and makes them happy, sad, or concerned. Photography should go beyond the surface facts of a story and capture the essence of a situation or personality.

Photo editors should be encouraging photographers never to shoot the mundane in a mundane way but rather to bring something a little extra, an insight using a candid human moment, no matter how routine the assignment. The best way to ensure active photography is for the photo editor to be involved early in the story-planning process.

The Professional Couple (Passive Image)

Louis DeLuca, The *Dallas Morning News*.

However, in spite of its limitations, there are times when passive photography is all that is required of a situation. Passive photography is all that is possible when the event that makes up the action of the story is no longer taking place. This is when the photographer makes the best of the situation and produces the best possible environmental portrait. These are legitimate and useful roles for passive photography to play.

PHOTO EDITOR AS GATEKEEPER

The photo editor has a very important role to play: that of a gatekeeper of the integrity of photojournalism. Under no circumstances should passive photography be manipulated to suggest to the reader that it is active. Why not set up photographs to make them more visually interesting? Because the very existence of newspapers and newsmagazines depends on the reader's belief that those newspapers and magazines tell the truth about the events described in their pages. Photography must be held to the same level of veracity as the rest of the newspaper.

USING THE PHOTOGRAPH IN THE CORRECT CONTEXT

Photographers and photo editors must strive to give an accurate image of an event or person rather than taking a minor incident out of context because it makes a nice photo. They must not present to the reader an aberration, a fleeting moment unlike the rest of what was documented. It is not fair to publish tears of joy as if they were tears of anguish. It is not truthful for a photographer or photo editor to select a strong image even though it is not indicative of what the photographer found at the event.

In addition, computers and electronic imaging equipment make it possible to easily manipulate images without leaving a trace. The photo editor plays a very important role in protecting the integrity of the photograph, both within and outside the photo department. Photojournalism can never lose the reader's trust.

One of the most significant things that a photo editor can do to improve the photographic report at any newspaper is to ban the use of the word *art* as a descriptor of the photography that goes into the newspaper. It is not the term

from the Photo Desk

Figure 6.12 ■ Figure 6.13 ■ Figure 6.14 ■ Figure 6.15

Traditional film editing is still done at the light table. Working as a team, the photo editor and the photographer decide which images complement the narrative and visually tell the story. This is when cropping and caption information should be discussed.

FIGURE 6.12

Working at the Light Table

Andrew Scott, The *Dallas Morning News.*

FIGURE 6.13

Taking a Closer Look

Andrew Scott, The *Dallas Morning News.*

itself that is so detrimental but rather the set of attitudes behind the word. When photojournalism is called art, the term implies that it is essentially decorative in function. That's an incorrect and dangerous assumption. Though much news photography has artistic qualities, it is not decoration; it is news information, just as narrative is information, but information that presents itself to the reader in a unique way. Communication is the prime function of pictures in journalism.

SHEPHERDING THE USE OF PHOTOGRAPHS

Two of the most important functions of photo editors are film editing and shepherding photo use throughout the newspaper. Although there are general rules for both, there are no absolutes. Photography is subjective, and always has been, and always will be. It doesn't take attending too many news budget meetings or watching too many photo contest judgings to confirm that. Figures 6.12 through 6.15 show the editing process for both traditional film and digital images.

Digital photography is edited on the computer screen rather than the light table. It can be done the same as traditional contact sheets, in which many images at a time are viewed or as a single image that fills the screen. Regardless of the method, traditional film editing and digital photo editing have the same goal in mind: finding the best content appropriate for the published story. After cropping and caption information are discussed, it becomes the photo editor's job to protect the vision of the photographer so that it is published properly.

FIGURE 6.14

Discussing Photo Editing

Andrew Scott, The *Dallas Morning News.*

FIGURE 6.15

Editing Photo on Computer Screen

Andrew Scott, The *Dallas Morning News.*

Photographs provide information, generate an aesthetic appreciation, and evoke an emotional response. At their best, photographs give the reader an immediate, deeply felt insight into the news and generate an almost visceral response to an event or individual.

Photographs that are only informational are plain basic reporting. Just as in narrative, a photograph can have all the necessary information but can be boring. People don't read boring stories, and they don't look at mundane photographs. If the reader is not engaged, that reader is lost. Purely informational photographs are the very last choice.

John Steinbeck and Ernest Hemingway never published a book without an editor. Photojournalists, like writers, benefit greatly from an editor. It can be a love–hate relationship but more often than not, the result is better work.

There are times when photographers get so emotionally involved in a shoot or a project that they might not approach the photo-editing process as objectively as they should.

When photographers cover an event, a situation, or a person, they are seeing and hearing far more than what they frame in their camera. Sometimes it is very hard not to subconsciously include what they know when looking at film during the editing process. A frame may have much more meaning to the photographer because of this peripheral information. The photo editor, like the reader, can glean only that information present in the image. The photo editor is looking at the film and assisting in the selection process with the reader in mind.

THE PHOTOGRAPHER AND PHOTO EDITOR WORKING SIDE BY SIDE

There will be times when a photographer is still on location at deadline and will have to do his or her own editing, a situation that has become much more common with the proliferation of digital cameras.

However, the optimal method is having the photographer and photo editor work side by side. At the *Dallas Morning News*, the system is for the photographer to make the initial edit and selections. The reasoning for this is that the photographer was the reporter in the field and witnessed the event or subject. The photographer then re-edits with a photo editor when the entire assignment is discussed, the final frame or frames are picked, and the optimal cropping of the image is decided. All assignments are edited in this way, even simple portraits, because this is one of the best places for coaching by the photo editor to take place. Images transmitted by the photographer from location are subject to the same editing policy at a later time. This ensures that a photographer and a photo editor talk about almost every assignment. It is a very good way to keep a sense of direction in the photography department and ensure a consistent daily visual report.

Good photographers never cover the routine in a mundane way. They will at the very least try to add to the aesthetic appeal using graphics, composition, quality of light, framing, camera angle, and the like. However, there is a tendency for these approaches to be overused and become cliches. The photo editor can control this by a simple rule that will cut down on this repetition: Remember what was published yesterday, what will be published today, and what might be published tomorrow.

The images for which the photographer and the photo editor are ultimately looking are those that evoke an emotional response—photographs that make the reader happy or sad, laugh or cry, or get angry. These are the images that make a difference and are what photographers should always strive to achieve.

To achieve meaningful photographs and produce visual storytelling images, photographers use many techniques that should be discussed both inside and outside the photo department in visual terms. The visual language previously mentioned uses terms that allow a photo editor to discuss the value of an image during the editing process and outside the photo department when photo usage is discussed. Figures 6.16 through 6.21 are meaningful storytelling photos that provide examples of what good photo editors look for.

from the Photo Desk

Figure 6.16 ■ Figure 6.17 ■ Figure 6.18

Photographs that capture the emotion of the subject or an event give the reader an immediate, deeply felt insight into the news, generating an almost visceral response to the event or individual.

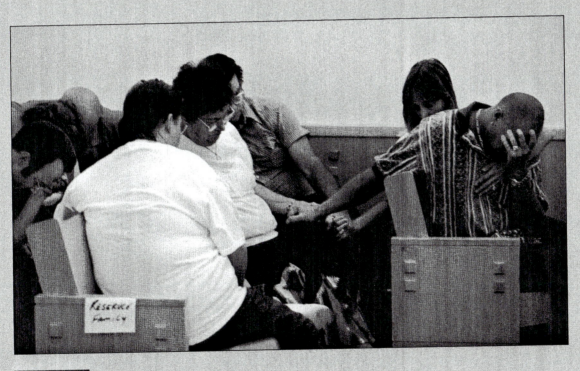

FIGURE 6.16

Prayer before the Verdict

In the courtroom, a family says a prayer moments before the jury found a family member guilty of aggravated kidnapping of a 6-year-old girl. It addresses what the families go through, not only the victim's family but also that of the accused, during a criminal trial.

David Woo, The *Dallas Morning News*.

FIGURE 6.17

Anger during a Ku Klux Klan Rally

An individual voicing her extreme displeasure at a Ku Klux Klan rally depicts the extreme emotion people feel toward the organization.

David Leeson, The *Dallas Morning News.*

FIGURE 6.18

Relatives of the *Kursk* Submarine Crew

The photograph of an elderly Russian submariner hugging a girl at a naval base brought home the grief of family and friends left behind after the submarine disaster. Relatives of the *Kursk* crew were brought to the site in the Barents Sea where 118 sailors died aboard the Russian submarine in 2000, to give them a chance to pay their respects to their dead relatives.

Yuri Kochetkov, Agence Presse France.

from the Photo Desk

Figure 6.19 ■ Figure 6.20 ■ Figure 6.21

Some of the most successful photographs are those that capture subjects in their most intimate moments. It puts the reader into the scene, to view the subject as a fly on the wall would. Intimate images are the basis for documentary photography and allow the reader to feel empathy with another human being and have a better understanding of the human condition.

FIGURE 6.19

Ballet Contestants Awaiting Tryouts

The photograph of the young ballet contestants waiting to try out for the Nutcracker is a delightful look at four young girls being themselves. While one tries to remain aloof to it all, another shows her anxiety at competing, as the other two posture as to who is better. This is a delightful intimate moment that says far more about human beings than the actual competition.

Gayle Shomer, The *Charlotte Observer.*

FIGURE 6.20

Fleeing Kosovo

Having lived in a wagon since fleeing Kosovo, an Albanian woman cuts her husband's hair as their child looks on in 1999. The photograph allows the reader to enter their "living room" and gives a better understanding of the Balkan conflict.

Joel Robine, Agence Presse France.

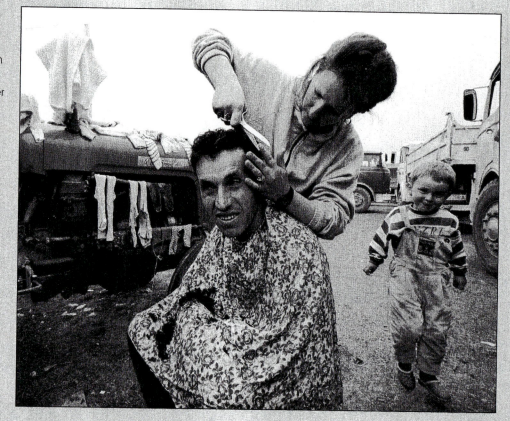

FIGURE 6.21

Brother and Sister Tiff

What person can't identify with a family tiff as is so intimately captured in this image of a brother and sister facing off while waiting for the school bus near their home?

Gayle Shomer, The Charlotte Observer.

CROPPING AND CAPTION WRITING

Photo editors should be involved in two areas that sometimes do not receive enough attention: cropping and caption writing.

Cropping

When covering events, rarely can news photographers frame the image exactly the way they want. There are too many variables—subjects moving, lens selection, camera angle, quality of light, and background, to mention a few. Much of the time, a photographer can only loosely frame the image and must rely on cropping later. Rarely does a photographer nail an uncroppable image. Photographers and photo editors should always include a discussion of cropping as part of the film-editing process. Figures 6.22 through 6.30 show examples of both good and bad crops.

from the Photo Desk
Figure 6.22 ■ Figure 6.23 ■
Figure 6.24 ■ Figure 6.25

Good cropping depends on knowing what information is essential and what is dispensable in order to best tell the story with impact. The impact of the basketball overhead shot is greatly improved by eliminating the two players who are having no effect on the play.

FIGURE 6.22

Overhead Shot

Louis DeLuca, The *Dallas Morning News.*

FIGURE 6.23

Overhead Shot before Cropping

Louis DeLuca, The *Dallas Morning News.*

FIGURE 6.24

Distance Shot

Chris Gerald, Agence
Presse France.

There are times when
things are happening
so quickly and unex-
pectedly that photo-
graphers can only
frame on the run and
crop for effect later.
The photographer
who shot the Pales-
tinian youth proudly
showing Israeli blood
on his hands as he is
cheered by fellow
protesters had only
a moment to photo-
graph the youth as
he briefly appeared
at the window. He
shot what he could
with the lens he
had available and
was able to come
up with a dramatic
shot by cropping
the image later.

FIGURE 6.25

**Distance Shot
after Cropping**

Chris Gerald, Agence
Presse France.

from the Photo Desk

Figure 6.26 ■ Figure 6.27 ■ Figure 6.28

By cropping in tight on the young Congolese boys' faces, the impact is increased and the military presence is retained in the picture. The storytelling power of the baseball image is greatly increased by eliminating all but the fan who caught the ball and the visiting team player walking dejectedly away. The tight crop on the women during a baptism heightens the emotional impact of the ceremony.

FIGURE 6.26

Young Congolese Boys

Barbara Davidson, The *Dallas Morning News*.

FIGURE 6.27
Catching the Game Ball
Louis DeLuca, The *Dallas Morning News*.

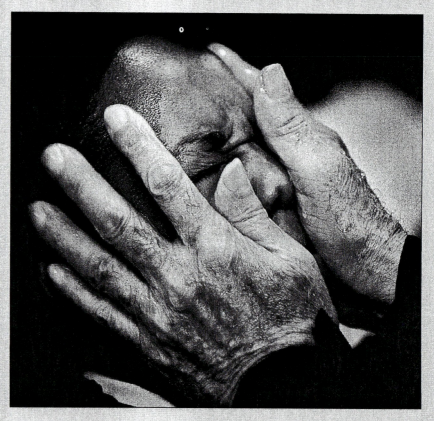

FIGURE 6.28
Baptism Ceremony
Patrick Schneider, The *Charlotte Observer*.

from the Photo Desk

Figure 6.29 ■ Figure 6.30

It is important to remember that although the photograph is usually the first thing the reader sees, there is a lot of competition on the page. Photos should be cropped for the optimal effect. If it had been cropped tighter, the photograph of the young female soldier going off to the Gulf War would have been more effective and a quicker read without loss of pertinent information.

FIGURE 6.29

Soldiers Going off to the Gulf War

Paula Nelson, The *Dallas Morning News.*

FIGURE 6.30

Female Soldier Going off to the Gulf War

Paula Nelson, The *Dallas Morning News.*

Simply stated, photographs are rectangles that contain information, and it is the information the photo editor and photographer decide to include that determines the shape of the photograph. Cropping can help an image, but if not done well, it can also hurt the image. The key to good cropping is to recognize what is indispensable and what can be done to the image to emphasize the message of the photograph. When it is done poorly, the point of the photograph will be lost, and its communicative powers will be greatly diminished. There is an optimal crop for every photograph.

Cropping can also add impact to the image and draw the reader in. By cropping out unnecessary information, the entry point can be emphasized, resulting in greater impact. When clarity of information and optimal impact of the image are achieved, a successful crop has been made.

Most people are familiar with the Chinese proverb "A picture is worth a thousand words." In truth, that is very rarely the case. Angus McDougall says in his book *Visual Impact in Print* that in using photographs, communication is best achieved when pictures and words reinforce each other, when they work in concert.

Photo editors must fight the occasional designer who tries to dictate the size and shape in a preordained layout. Photographs should never be used to fill holes on the page. Content should always dictate the design.

Captions/Cutlines

One of the stepchildren of the newspaper and other publications is the caption, also called a cutline. The Poynter Institute's eye tracking study concludes that often the first text read on a page is the cutline of the lead photograph. Yet captions more often than not receive the least amount of time and effort. Many times, they merely state what readers can already see for themselves, doing nothing to advance the photograph or the story. Figure 6.31 shows good and bad caption examples.

Paula LaRocque, an assistant managing editor and writing coach at the *Dallas Morning News* and author of *Championship Writing*, says that *eye-catching,*

FIGURE 6.31

Convicted Child Molester

Photo captions should go beyond stating the obvious. The photographer must be responsible for the reporting. The caption written for this photograph of a just-convicted child molester went beyond the 5 W's.

As the photograph was made, the man said, "I think I have been through five years of hell already. I have lost everything. I have lost my friends. I have lost my self-respect. I lost my dignity. I lost everything." When that quote is added to the caption, the reader has a better understanding of the extreme anguish on the man's face.

Andrew Scott, The *Dallas Morning News*.

unfortunately for writers, means almost anything but text—headlines, decks, or other enlarged or specialty type; photos and photo captions; art and graphics; design elements such as white space and bullets.

She says that writers often resent the attention given to nontextual elements. They will fight for every scrap of space to write a longer story. But that's a self-defeating impulse. Writers who know how to be their own best friends will not try to take space from other elements but will try instead to *make* space for them. They know that those elements will bring the readers into their stories as fat chunks of gray type never will.

LaRocque says that even casual readers look at captions and might or might not read the story based on their attractiveness, readability, and interest. Yet captions are often weakly written.

Although photographs are taken before their captions are written, it is common to write in the present tense to emphasize the immediacy of the image. LaRocque says that pairing a present tense verb with a past tense time element is one of the most common problems in caption writing. One couldn't say—at least, not grammatically—that the new mayor *is* sworn in last week, that a mother *holds* her son yesterday, or that an officer *carries* a child to safety Wednesday. Yet the following captions were published:

"Lee P. Brown *is* sworn in by U.S. District Judge Vanessa Gilmore to become Houston's mayor Friday."

"Guadalupe Truimo *holds* her 3-year-old son, Jose Marco, while he *is* hooked up to a kidney dialysis machine at Children's Medical Center on *Wednesday*."

"A SWAT team *carries* 7-year-old Jamia Lipscomb to safety *Wednesday* at the end of a nearly 42-hour standoff in McKinney."

Newspaper captions often cook up this sort of sequence-of-tense hash in an attempt to add to the immediacy of the photograph. La Rocque thinks that captions should be written in the natural form, as in the following examples:

"was sworn in Friday,"

"held her son Wednesday,"

"carried Jamia to safety Wednesday."

There is more to writing good captions than mechanical accuracy, of course. Their eye-catching visibility demands grace, color, and information as well. In other words, once the photo engages the eye, the caption should engage the mind.

Captions are a wonderful place to go beyond what the reader can already see for himself or herself. It can add information to the story, it can reinforce a point of view or message, and it can complement the text.

It all has to start with the photographer, for after all he or she is the one on the scene. There are times when the traditional 5 W's—who, what, when, where and why—are not enough, and there are times when they are not necessary.

There are some general rules in good caption writing. It is important to have the final cropped version of the image in front of the person who is writing the final caption. If the final version is not used, you run the risk of directing the reader's attention to something that is no longer in the frame.

Good captions should do the following:

- Point out subtleties that might not be apparent to the casual viewer
- Point out ambiguities and prevent possible reader misunderstanding
- Use quotes that add depth to the image and its storytelling power
- Explain technical information about photographs that use special effects
- Relate to the four nonvisual senses that are integral to the image: hearing, smell, taste, and touch

- Explain what happened before and after the photo was taken to give it context
- Explain what is not apparent to the reader

A good caption should not do the following:

- State only the obvious, which results in repetition
- Raise more questions than answers and leave the reader confused
- Change the original message or point of view of the photographer
- Tell the reader how a subject is feeling or thinking unless he or she is quoted
- Overlook the mood of the photo—don't write a flip or humorous caption for a serious situation.

THE IMPORTANCE OF PHOTOGRAPHY

Photography is an essential element in the mix of ingredients that comprise the daily newspaper. It is essential because of the power it is capable of bringing to the presentation of the news but also for the simple reason that readers like photographs and are drawn to them.

Research conducted by the Poynter Institute and others tell us the readership of photographs is higher than that of any other element in the newspaper. A photograph is typically the first element readers see on the page. Many writers have learned that readership of stories and even headlines are greater if photographs accompany them. Writers also know that one of the best ways to get on the front page is to have good photography with their story.

Photo editors and photographers can choose the best frame during the editing process. They can make the optimal crop and write a thoughtful and concise caption. They can process the photo to make it technically perfect. But that is never enough. A photograph is judged by what hits the reader's doorstep, and here is where a photo editor has an important role to play.

On the one hand, one of the photo editor's functions is to protect the vision of the photographer once the editing session is completed. On the other hand, and more important, the photo editor needs to serve the reader.

Just as stories need to be read to communicate, so do photographs. If the reader cannot access the information, the photograph has failed in its essential function: to communicate.

It is the photo editor's job to ensure that photographs are used in the newspaper in a manner that allows them to be read by the reader. More often than not, this means the size of a photograph on the page. With stories, photos, captions, headlines, and graphics there is a tremendous competition for space on any given page. This will become more intense as newspapers convert to the 50-inch printing web which gives the newspaper page 7% less space to work with than the traditional page.

There was a period in the late 1970s and 1980s when many photo editors thought that good photo use was to run huge photographs, to the point of trying to make some pages look like posters. Today, most photo editors take a much more thoughtful and journalistic approach. They know that it is all about storytelling. They realize that some images with a great deal of detail or subtle information might need to run large while many photographs that are a quick read may run smaller. Generally speaking, readership is higher with larger photographs, but photo editors also know that rarely does a routine photograph look better if it is run larger. Figures 6.32 through 6.51 are examples of good and bad photo use in terms of sizing, visual variety, photo pairing, stories and essays.

from the Photo Desk

Figure 6.32 ■ Figure 6.33

Having a dominant image on the page adds impact not only to the image but also to the page and draws the reader into the stories. The secondary images should be of sizes that don't compete with the lead photograph for the reader's attention. When the dominant photograph is small, the result is a very gray and uninviting page.

FIGURE 6.32

Austin American-Statesman Page

Austin American-Statesman.

FIGURE 6.33

Dallas Morning News Page

The *Dallas Morning News.*

from the Photo Desk

Figure 6.34

A photographer needs to have a sequence in mind while shooting out in the field. Rarely can a coherent sequence be put together as an afterthought back in the office. The key to editing a sequence is to edit tightly and not try to tell too much. Recognizing the possibility of a sequence, the photographer covering a local fire department's practice drill with a donated house shot everything from the same position. The photo editor pared it down to three images, giving the reader an interesting look at the exercise from start to finish.

FIGURE 6.34

Photo Sequence

Joe Stefanchik, The *Dallas Morning News*.

For practice purposes

The Sunnyvale Fire Department recently set up practice drills at a donated house on Barnes Bridge Road. After the utilities are shut off, the structure is set ablaze. Officials say that in such drills, bigger is better. As Sunnyvale Fire Chief Mike Magee says, "You never know when you're going to come across the big one. We train for the worst and hope for the best."

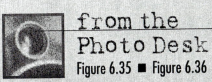

There are times when pairing two photographs that complement each other can tell the story better than just one image. The aerial photograph of a tornado's swath across a community is a dramatic shot of the destruction. By adding the photograph of the Red Cross worker comforting one of the victims in an emergency shelter, the photo editor has added the human element to the visual coverage.

FIGURE 6.35
Tornado Damage

David Leeson, The *Dallas Morning News*.

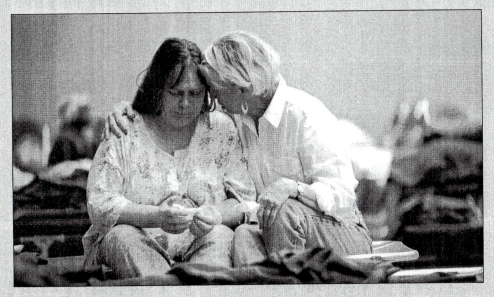

FIGURE 6.36
Comforting a Victim

Jim Mahoney, The *Dallas Morning News*.

from the Photo Desk

Figure 6.37

By pairing photographs of the final play of the Super Bowl where the losing team comes up short with the emotion of the winning coach, the photo editor has been able to tell an important story about the game. The headline is written for the lead photograph and increases the effectiveness of the package.

FIGURE 6.37

Rams Win the Super Bowl

The *Dallas Morning News.*

from the Photo Desk

Figure 6.38 ■ Figure 6.39 ■ Figure 6.40 ■ Figure 6.41 ■
Figure 6.42 ■ Figure 6.43 ■ Figure 6.44

Photography does not necessarily have to mirror the narrative but rather can complement and reinforce the story, thus increasing the storytelling quality of the package. Cheryl Diaz Meyer had an assignment to photograph a new methadone treatment center. The photo request suggested that one or two images were needed and warned that faces could not be shown. Recognizing the visual limitations, Cheryl took a different approach and found a young fourth-generation heroin addict just starting treatment at the center who was willing to be photographed. By photographing one individual in depth, Cheryl was able to put a human face on the story and give the readers a better understanding of heroin addiction and the need for methadone clinics.

FIGURE 6.38

Tears ran down Brandi's youthful cheeks as she sat in her car, overwhelmed by her heroin addiction.
Cheryl Diaz Meyer, The *Dallas Morning News*.

FIGURE 6.39

After melting heroin in water and "cooking" it in a spoon over a lighter, Brandi filled up a needle.

Cheryl Diaz Meyer, The *Dallas Morning News*.

FIGURE 6.40

In the privacy of her grandparents' bathroom, Brandi injected heroin into her jugular vein rather than her arm because of collapsed veins.

Cheryl Diaz Meyer, The *Dallas Morning News*.

FIGURE 6.41

In a fit of craving, Brandi sold her grandmother's VCR to a friend to support her heroin habit.

Cheryl Diaz Meyer,
The *Dallas Morning News*.

FIGURE 6.42

A counselor at the methadone clinic discussed options in dealing with Brandi's continued use of heroin.

Cheryl Diaz Meyer,
The *Dallas Morning News*.

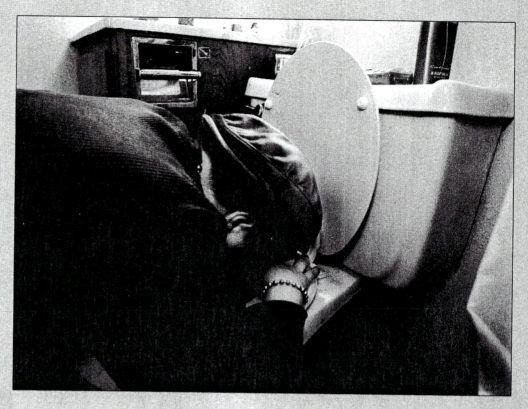

from the Photo Desk

Figure 6.45 ■ Figure 6.46 ■ Figure 6.47 ■ Figure 6.48 ■
Figure 6.49 ■ Figure 6.50 ■ Figure 6.51

Photographer Joe Stefanchik was sent with a writer to Angola
when his newspaper decided to do a story on the horrible
toll land mines were taking on civilian populations around the
world. Several days into the trip, Joe decided that not only did
he want to complement and enhance the writer's story with his
images, but he also wanted to do his own interpretive photo
essay on the subject. He wanted to explain and explore the
problems of civilians and land mines, not just in Angola, but
around the world as well.

He framed most of his photographs in such a way that
people were partially or fully faceless because he wanted to
deemphasize the specific individuals he was photographing
and emphasize individuals universally.

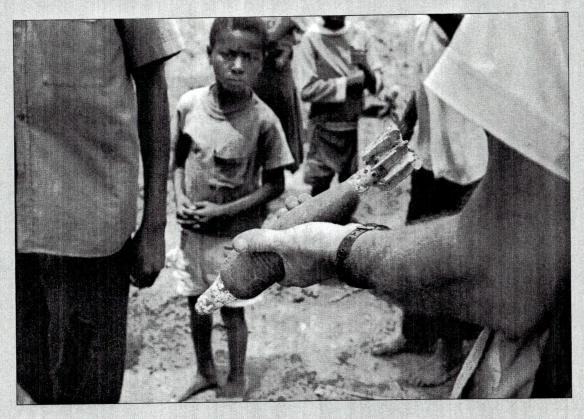

FIGURE 6.45

A demolition expert holds a live 82mm mortar found by a child in an Angolan village.
Joe Stefanchik, The *Dallas Morning News*.

FIGURE 6.46

The man in the foreground lost both legs after an injury from an antitank mine, and the man in the background lost his leg to an antipersonnel mine.

Joe Stefanchik, The *Dallas Morning News*.

FIGURE 6.47

Two years after the civil war ended, people walk to the market in town making sure not to step off the road.

Joe Stefanchik, The *Dallas Morning News*.

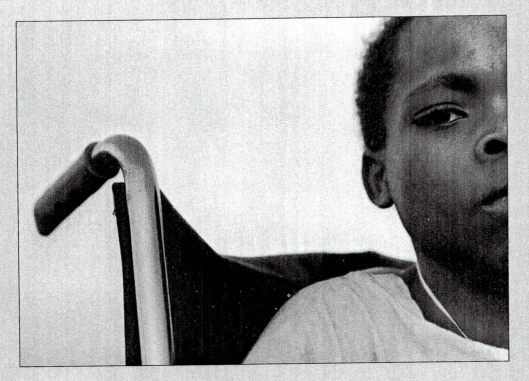

This young boy was injured by an antipersonnel mine while playing with friends, resulting in the amputation of his right leg.

Joe Stefanchik, The *Dallas Morning News*.

This young mother lost her leg to an antipersonnel mine while walking back to her home from the market.

Joe Stefanchik, The *Dallas Morning News*.

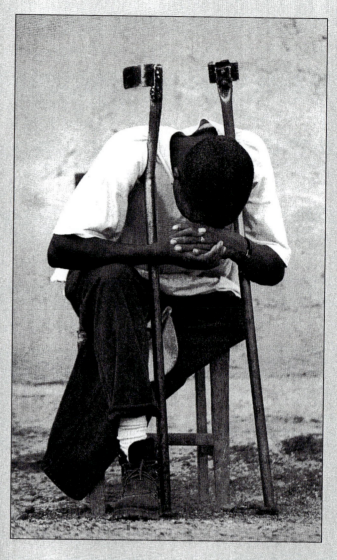

Photo editors should always attempt to find the best way to tell the story. They must decide when a single images works best and when a supporting image or images are needed to best visually tell the complete story. There will be times when the words do the best job, or an infographic, or—more often than not—a combination. Rarely does a photograph stand alone, but there will be occasions when the photographs take the lead and have the most storytelling capability, and the writer needs to be able to accommodate the images to the point of sometimes changing the story line.

Photo editors must always be sensitive to both the readers and the subjects. Research has shown that most editors, both word and visual, are more willing to publish distressing or troublesome photographs than readers are to view them.

It has been said that a good newspaper is society's mirror. Unfortunately, bad things happen around the world, every day. Editors should never publish photographs just for shock value. Photographers can't, nor should they, make a plane crash look pleasant, but editors don't have to publish close-ups of bodies. However, there are times when the horror of the photograph is

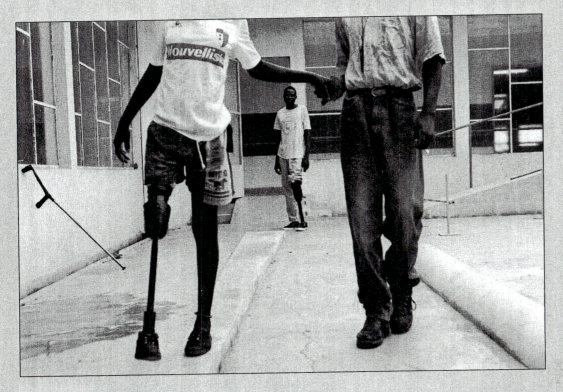

FIGURE 6.51

Mine victims learn to use prostheses with the help of a physiotherapist.

Joe Stefanchik, The *Dallas Morning News*.

appropriate to the horror of the event. Photo editors can't clean up reality to the point at which accidents are bloodless, death does not cause tears, and pain does not hurt. But they should make every effort to report the news and still be sensitive to the readers, and they should let their subjects keep their dignity.

Many disturbing photographs are published in newspapers ever year. The bombing of the Alfred P. Murrah Federal Building in Oklahoma City (Figure 6.52), the shootings at Columbine High School (Figure 6.53), and the collapse of the bonfire at Texas A&M (Figure 6.54) are recent examples. Photo editors should immediately flags photographs like this and bring them to the attention of senior management.

It is responsible journalism to publish photographs like this of important events. There are times when we need to show our readers things they might not want to see but need to see to understand the human tragedy that is part of life. However, photo editors should never make these decisions in a vacuum. It is not responsible journalism to publish disturbing photographs without serious discussion in the newsroom with the reader's sensitivity in mind.

from the Photo Desk

Figure 6.52 ■ Figure 6.53 ■ Figure 6.54

Many images in news photography have become cultural icons because of their impact and universal appeal. As such, they define a particular event in an indelible manner and convey meaning that goes well beyond the purely specific.

FIGURE 6.52

Baby Baylee at the Oklahoma City Bombing

Oklahoma City fire captain Chris Fields carrying the lifeless body of one-year-old Baylee Almon, who was killed in the bombing at the Alfred P. Murrah Federal Building in downtown Oklahoma City.

Charles Porter IV, Corbis Sygma.

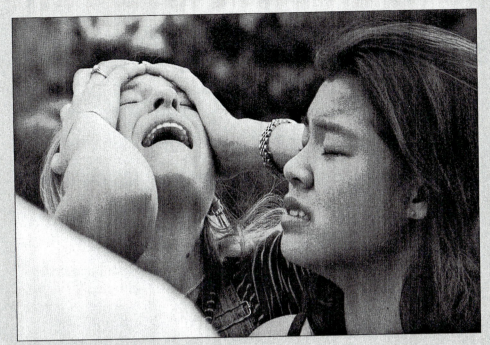

Shooting at Columbine

At the mention of Columbine High School in Littleton, Colorado, most people will immediately visualize the two young women students reacting at a triage scene after two students opened fire at the suburban Denver high school, killing twelve students and a teacher before killing themselves.

George Kochaniec, *Denver Rocky Mountain News,* Corbis Sygma.

Texas A&M Bonfire Collapse

The tragic collapse of the forty-foot high pyramid of logs built for the annual University of Texas–Texas A&M football game, which killed 12 students, produced the iconic image of the young student trapped in the middle of the log pile.

J. P. Beato, *The Battalion.*

THE HIERARCHY FOR VISUAL JOURNALISTS

For a long time there was believed to be a glass ceiling for visual journalists; it was thought that they couldn't get out from under the visual umbrella and move up in the management hierarchy in the newsroom. For the most part, this was true.

But that is all changing, and the instrument of change was the evolution of the photo editor. Over the last decade, many photo editors have proved to be excellent journalists and have shown that they can successfully manage people, space, dollars, and ideas.

Another recent development that has increased the photo editor's value in the newsroom is technology. Newsroom editors of the future will need the technological skills that many photo editors are pioneering today. Photo editors have taken computers well beyond the function of word processing. They were, after all, the people who brought the digital world into the newsroom.

Gannett, the largest newspaper group in the United States, and Scripps Howard Newspapers have led the way in the promotion and outside hiring of visual editors into the managing editor ranks of their newspapers.

Their philosophy on filling editing positions is the same as their philosophy on filling staff positions: Find diversity of backgrounds to become more responsive and reflective of the community's diversity. This translates into promoting editors from all ranks of the newsroom.

Ralph Langer, retired executive editor and senior vice president of the *Dallas Morning News* and current journalism department chair at Southern Methodist University, points out that a balance is needed and will be ever more critical to people who aspire to be leaders in newsrooms. Competition at this level is intense because the opportunities are fewer. Someone with strong skills in one area but largely undeveloped or undemonstrated skills in other areas will face stiff competition from people who are better balanced.

Training and knowledge lead to confidence, something that many good visual editors lack when it comes to managing outside their departments. Visual editors need to place themselves in situations in which they can develop this confidence.

A photo editor who feels deficient in certain skills should seek out opportunities to cross-train in other departments and ask to be invited to meetings where he or she can become more versed in how the paper is produced. Photo editors need to be bilingual, to be able to participate in conversations about things other than just photography, to think beyond their individual department—in particular, about the news events themselves.

One of the best examples of cross-training from a visual department is David Yarnold at the *San Jose Mercury News*. In the late 1970s Yarnold was a photographer and photo editor of the *Daily News* in Longview, Washington. Today Yarnold is the executive editor at the *Mercury News*. Bruce Baumann, managing editor of the *Evansville* [Indiana] *Courier & Press*, and Randy Cochran, head of operations for Scripps Howard, both rose from the ranks of the photography department.

Future photo editors will be people who are grounded in the full range of journalistic skills, not perfectly balanced but not just involved in photos entirely, or just words, or just graphics—or just technocrats. Those who are successful will be those who best blend journalistic and management skills. Photo editors can help to make newspapers better, more relevant, and critical to people's lives.

AREAS FOR DISCUSSION

- Outline the terms listed in the chapter that are used for a visual language. Bring photographs illustrating one or more of these terms.

- Discuss the importance of photo editors and photographers working side by side. Interview photo editors and photographers from various size newspapers to discuss this working situation.

- Compare the use of photographs in a newspaper that publishes on the web and one that publishes in traditional print. Note whether the same photographs are used for a story in both publishing formats. Compare the play of photographs in each format.

chapter 7

Transmitting in the Field

Whether the photographer is working as a freelance or staff photojournalist, there are many occasions when the photographic image must be sent either from the location where the event was photographed or from another remote site. As in all other work processes within the field of photojournalism discussed in this book, new tools have created new methods. Digital technology has created vast changes in the process of transmission.

As a result, not only has the old way changed but a variety of different methods of transmission have been created. The tools, skills, hardware, and software needed for transmission will depend on the news publication's preferred transmission method, location, and time.

A Bit of Background

From the 1930s to the 1980s, transmitting technology changed very little. The transmission process employed a simple machine to transmit the visual information from a photographic print over telephone wires. This cumbersome and time-consuming method required darkroom facilities at the remote site to make the print. Then the print was taped to a spinning drum, and a photocell read the light reflected off the print and transmitted this information.

By the mid-1980s advances in technology made it possible to transmit photographic information by scanning the negative, eliminating the process and time of making a transmission print. One of the first of these types of scanning systems was the Leafax transmitter, which was made available from Leaf Systems or the Associated Press. The portable scanning/transmission station fit in a suitcaselike carrying case and was run by a computer.

Shortly after this development in scanning and transmission technology, other systems were created and introduced to the professional market. Most notable was the system that combined a Macintosh PowerBook with a Nikon Coolscan. As laptop computer and scanning technology continues to evolve, so will transmission methods. (See the book web site for updates on systems.)

TRANSMISSION METHODS

File Transfer Protocol (FTP)

File transfer protocol (FTP) is the most prevalent means of photo delivery. It is direct and immediate. The status of information flow can be monitored as the bits of information travel to the intended destination. The computer screen window shows the number of bits from source to destination. Ken Geiger, director of photography for the *Dallas Morning News,* says that physically and psychologically, this is a very important factor when working under event and deadline pressure. Sending the digital image file via an FTP site is a much "cleaner" system than e-mailing the file.

Another factor that makes FTP the preferred method of transmitting photographic images is the fact the digital image file format is not limited to the JPEG compression format. Also, complete pages (for example, a section front) can be saved in a PDF (portable document file), keeping text, photographs, and layout intact.

Bulletin Board System (BBS)

A bulletin board system (BBS) allows the image to be posted at a particular site for the photo editor of the publication to retrieve as needed. This system can be used as a backup to FTP. As the Internet evolves, this system is becoming obsolete.

E-Mail

Although convenient and used by news publications of all sizes to receive photographic images, e-mail is the most unreliable method. Problems with servers sending and receiving the e-mail, e-mail attachment viruses, and differences in computer platforms are just a few issues that occur when using the e-mail system to send photographic image files.

Cellular Phone Transmission

The first rule of thumb in using cellular phone for transmission is to turn the phone off before connecting. The second rule of thumb is to make sure you have the appropriate adapter. Adapters are a problem only if you don't have them. The biggest problem with foreign photo transmissions is the quality of the phone lines. This is where a BBS using Zterm is of benefit; disconnects of transmissions can be resumed at the point at which they were cut off. If numerous transmissions are expected for many days, an account should be set up with a local Internet service provider (ISP). Dialing locally with the ISP to transmit via FTP is less problematic than using long distance (see Figures 7.1 and 7.2).

New services on the market will continue to offer better transmission speed than ordinary cell phones. The speed of wireless connections will continue to revolutionize transmission practices for photojournalists. Immediacy of transmission will be commonplace and not only associated with special assignments. The Web is the driving force for these developments.

- Locate electrical power and the phone line.
- Have the correct phone line adapter (if in another country).
- Know the phone number you are working from.
- Know whether the phone is pulse or tone.

FIGURE 7.1

Transmitting Tips

FIGURE 7.2

Satellite Transmission

Dallas Morning News staff members set up for satellite transmission from Cuba to Dallas during the Pope's visit to Cuba.

The *Dallas Morning News*.

THE NEW DAY

By Alan Greth, Executive Photo Editor, Contra Costa Times

Because the *Contra Costa Times* (a Knight-Ridder paper) is located in the San Francisco Bay area, we have the good fortune of having access to a wireless Internet network. All twenty-one of our staff photographers have Macintosh G3 PowerBooks with Ricochet wireless modems. These small modems provide a wireless Internet connection throughout most of our circulation area. As you can imagine, the D1 digital camera, the PowerBook, and the wireless modem make a potent combination. Not only does it enable us to beat our competition on deadline, but it has changed the way we all do our jobs.

As a former wire service photographer myself, I quickly realized the far-reaching impact these new tools have on the way we do our jobs. Staff photographers are no longer required to return to the office after shooting their assignments. Here at the *Times,* the shooters can retreat to a coffeeshop, their car, or anywhere else to edit and transmit their take. We use an FTP site to move the pictures back via our wireless Internet connections.

In fact, as I write this, I have a staff photographer on assignment some sixty-five miles from the paper. He will transmit from the field on this live news story. He lives near the assignment location. As you might imagine, he will be very happy to simply go home after he has transmitted his pictures. On this one assignment alone, this staffer will not have to drive 130 miles needlessly. This has dramatically changed my job, as well as those of the other picture editors.

AREAS FOR DISCUSSION

- Discuss various methods used to send photographs via the web.
- Discuss the psychological advantages and quality of the sent image file when using FTP instead of e-mailing the image.
- Call the photo directors of various sizes of newspapers and ask what method of transmission they are currently using.

chapter 8

ARCHIVING DIGITAL IMAGE FILES

Although most news publications continue to save photographic negatives or positives from a shooting assignment (when not shooting with digital cameras), the ability to file digital images in a database has revolutionized photographic assignment storage (now called archiving) and retrieval. With one keyword entered for a database search, numerous photographs can be retrieved in seconds. In the past, various filing systems were used to store negatives along with contact sheets from picture assignments. Usually, the negatives and contact sheets were filed by assignment date with the original picture assignment title (now called the *slug*). Publications continue to file negatives, which serve as a backup to the image database.

The electronic workflow system for archiving images will vary from one publication to another, depending on the software application that is used for the archiving database and how that particular publication handles dual publishing for traditional print and web.

Various software programs provide different features for captioning, proofing, saving, and retrieving photographic image files from the database. Some software applications work only as plug-ins with another program, such as Photoshop, to perform these functions; other applications work in addition to image-editing programs. Although this digital system has streamlined the image-archiving process, these archives or databases are also backed up by being burned to a CD (discussed later in the chapter) in addition to keeping the original negatives. This provides insurance against system crashes and lost or accidentally trashed files and alleviates system storage problems for large publications.

SOFTWARE

Software applications such as Extensis Portfolio, MediaStream, and Media Grid provide various methods of creating image databases. These databases are sometimes referred to as image libraries (see Figure 8.1). The software applications usually provide search, captioning, proofing, and browse features. Figure 8.2 shows the caption and photo information window for one program. However, some applications require a separate browser. (See the book web site for updates on current image archiving.)

FIGURE 8.1

North Texas Daily Photographic Archive

Photos by *North Texas Daily* staff photographers.

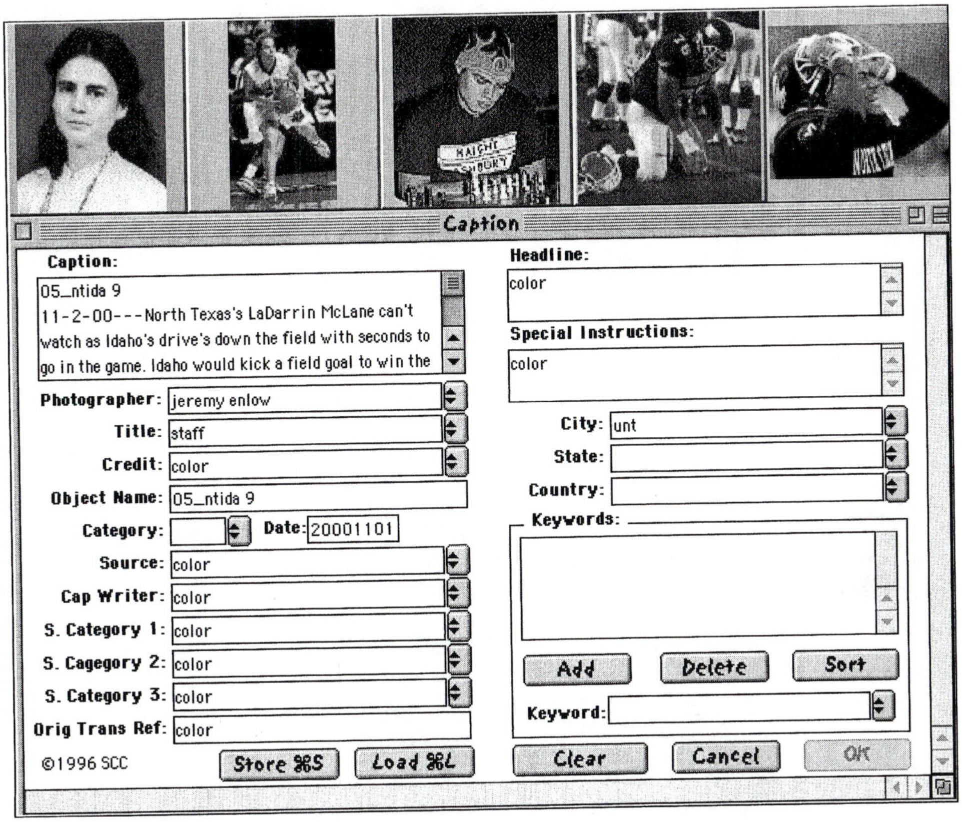

FIGURE 8.2

***North Texas Daily*
Photographic Archive
Caption and Photo
Information Window**

Photos by Jeremy Enlow,
North Texas Daily.

STANDARD FILE FORMAT FOR ARCHIVING
AND OTHER FEATURES

Most applications use JPEG as the standard file format to save photographic images for archiving and proofing. In addition to the features provided by a particular program that are listed above, some archiving software applications also provide tools to crop, edit the image and text, and create a format for photo assignments. If the software provides a function to create and format photo assignments, usually a feature will also allow for tracking the assignment through various stages of the workflow process.

This tracking process also automatically links all submitted image files with the original photo assignment for retrieval. Other information linked to the photographic image file includes various prepress information such as pixel dimensions and prepress settings. The photographer's name, assignment slug, assignment date and location, and any special instructions are also linked with the image file. (See the book web site for URL links to software demonstrations and updates.)

When the photographic digital file is archived in the image database library, separate catalogues can be created within the database. For example, all photographs can be stored in a catalogue separate from those for digital video or graphics files. *Catalogue* is the term used for the separate file folders of archived information. Cataloguing options can be set for each separate catalogue within the image database library.

- The photographer's name in the photographer field

- The negative file number in the credit field (Note: The negative file number is the number attached to the physical negative sleeve page that is filed in a binder or file cabinet.)

- The slug or title of the assignment in the JPEG name field

- The caption in the caption field

FIGURE 8.3

Information to Include with the Image File When Archiving

CAPTIONS AND ATTRIBUTE STORAGE

A very important feature that is necessary but not always provided in archiving software is the ability to link and store the caption or ITPC attributes for the image file. When selecting archiving, proofing, and browsing software applications, be aware of how the caption information is handled. Some programs require a separate plug-in to perform this function. These captioning plug-ins or applications will usually include a function that allows for automatic saving that attaches the .jpg extension to the image slug or title.

In most captioning software applications a screen information field provides space to list details about the image (see Figure 8.3). Figure 8.4 show a generic captioning window as used in Photoshop, Extensis, and other software applications.

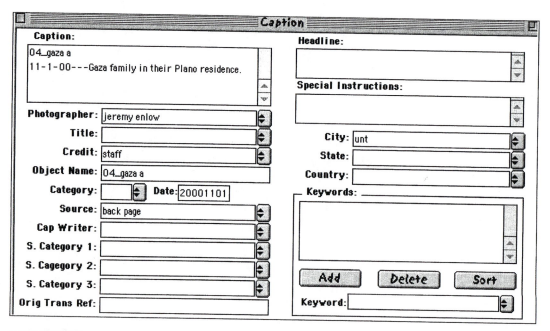

FIGURE 8.4

Captioning Window

A photo conversion utility usually allows for merging of photos and IPTC captions exported from an industry standard archive system such as Merlin (see the book web site for current information). Once merged with captions, images are saved as standard JPEG files complete with the embedded caption, ready for insertion into the database.

PROOFING

As was stated previously in the chapter, using an archiving software application or application plug-in that allows for image proofing is essential. By printing a hard copy of the image proof screen window, a paper trail is created for page editors or designers to refer to if the news publication is not completely paginated (see Figure 8.5). Compiling a notebook by date of all image proofs also provides a hard copy backup image library. As most publications move from the old school method of archiving to digital archiving, many photographers and editors want the ability to track images in traditional print and online (see Figure 8.5).

05_ntida 9
11-2-00---North Texas's LaDarrin McLane can't watch as Idaho's drive's down the field with seconds to go in the game. Idaho would kick a field goal to win the game with three seconds remaining to dash UNT's hope for a win.

FIGURE 8.5

Screen Image Proof

A screen image proof can be printed out to create a paper trail for non-paginated publications.

Photo by Jeremy Enlow, *North Texas Daily.*

SEARCHING THE ARCHIVE: DIGITAL IMAGE FILE AND/OR CD BACKUP

Most archiving software applications provide a variety of ways to search the archive. How to perform a search for a particular photograph will depend on what information was attached to the original digital photographic image file. For example, a keyword can be the photographer's name if the option to search under byline is chosen. Other searches can be conducted using the date of the assignment, assignment slug, or other information that might be included in the photograph's caption. Typical keyword searches include the byline, caption writer, city where the assignment took place, date of the assignment, file name (or assignment slug), and almost any information that is entered in the description field in archiving the photograph.

When launching a search, one specific catalogue can be searched at a time, or all catalogues within the image database archive can be searched at once. Duplicates in various catalogues can be identified and sorted.

If memory capacity and storage space are problems, portions of the image library database can be burned onto a CD and cleared from the database to provide room for new image files. When a search is conducted for an archived photograph that is not currently in the actual server database, the search will prompt the user to insert the archived CD to retrieve the photograph.

In addition to burning CDs to clear more storage space on a server hard drive, the negatives (if not shooting digitally) should be kept and filed as a backup.

INTRANET AND INTERNET ACCESS

Most archiving software supports access from a local Intranet via the web. For example, using any industry standard Internet browser, the image database library can be accessed on the web. Most digital archiving software provides the ability to search not only still digital image files, but archived digital and digitized video as well.

Some archiving software applications provide an enhanced web access function that also allows any document stored in the database to be marked for automated delivery to one or more destinations. Options provide the choice of transferring images and word documents to multiple destinations immediately or at some time in the future. In addition each destination can be preconfigured with a custom output template allowing for a variety of output formats, such as XML, HTML, NITF, and IPTC. Files can also be locked to limit access.

ARCHIVE DATABASE FOR TRADITIONAL PRINT PUBLICATION AND ONLINE

News publications generally customize their archiving system. In publishing dually—online and in traditional print—most professionals agree that the best system is to have one archive that serves both. This allows both publications to have access to all the information. As Keith Hitchens, director of photography of the *Fort Wayne News-Sentinel,* explains, "The web publication feeds off the traditional print newspaper archive for all images and all text enhancements for the web are also saved with archived images."

ARCHIVING MULTIMEDIA FORMATS

Archiving software should provide a function to insert multimedia files, including picture files, text files, portable document files (PDFs), sound (WAV) files, and video clips into the database. Ideally, the application will also allow browse and search functions throughout the database for all multimedia formats. As was discussed earlier in the chapter, most archiving software should in some way accommodate multi-media file formats, either by plug-in or within the application itself.

Because online publications use stills, video, and various multimedia formats, the archiving system for the web publication might vary and be totally separate from the traditional print publication.

For example, Washingtonpost-Newsweek interactive has a separate digital archive from the traditional print *Washington Post*. The online publication uses a series of CD-ROMs that can be linked together in a daisy chain on a jukebox player. This is necessary because of the multimedia content that is created independently of the printed newspaper.

Tom Kennedy, director of photography and design for washingtonpost. com, surmises that in the future, large publications that publish in both formats will probably unite all archives to provide for greater opportunity to facilitate the creation of new digital products. This will also allow for a business plan to facilitate syndication of individual images as well as content packages.

AREAS FOR DISCUSSION

- Compare and contrast image archiving using software to the old way of filing and organizing negatives and/or prints for reuse or reprint.
- Call various newspapers and find out who has the role of archiving staff photographers' digital image files.
- Discuss the importance of organizing digital image files for quick and easy retrieval to build portfolios and prepare contest entries.

chapter 9

SLIDE PORTFOLIOS

The portfolio is what you will be judged by, and there are many ways to prepare and present your work. In general, most photo directors, when surveyed, said that they still prefer to see work in slide form. However, it is recommended to send both slides and disks or CD-ROM portfolios. This way, knowledge of new technology is demonstrated, but the light table can be used when technology fails. Many professionals admitted that this happens a lot. Disks are sometimes hard to open, are slow, or are damaged when mailed. In addition, the portfolio can be seen more as a whole on the light table. Most photo directors stated that they receive about 50% disks and 50% slides, but it is best to send both. Preparing your portfolio for presentation on Zip disk, CD-ROM, and on the web is discussed in Chapter 10.

WHAT TO INCLUDE

A portfolio is a kind of living document. It should be representative of where a photojournalist is at the present time. Therefore, the portfolio should change to reflect the changes in the photojournalist. As photojournalists grow, their style changes, becoming more mature and focused. Strengths become more apparent, and technical skills improve. The photojournalist's visual voice becomes more pronounced.

What beginning photojournalists need to show a prospective employer is versatility, that they can handle a variety of situations and come back with a publishable photograph. A portfolio that has a lot of variety can reveal the potential of the photojournalist. For example, the portfolio should demonstrate that the photojournalist understands light, color, and has the ability to capture emotional impact. Much of this depends on the photojournalist's sense of timing, talent for visual framing, and knowledge of the tools (lens choice and use of depth of field) needed to document the moment.

When looking for a specialist—a sports shooter, for instance—a photo director will look for a photographer with a number of years of experience and a mature shooting style. So the beginning photojournalist must strive to show a variety of images (see Figure 9.1) and the ability to produce photo essays (see Figures 9.2 and 9.3). As a rule of thumb, there should be twenty to twenty-five singles and two photo stories/essays. The portfolio should also include spot news, general news, portraits, sports, and features. Mediocre photographs should not be included to attain this number. It is better to have fewer excel-

FIGURE 9.1

Thumbnails of Portfolio Singles

Amy Smotherman.

FIGURE 9.2

Thumbnails of a Portfolio Photo Essay

Amy Smotherman.

FIGURE 9.3

Thumbnails of a Portfolio Photo Essay

Amy Smotherman.

lent images that represent the photojournalist's current skill. Including weaker images only shows the photo editor or photo director that this photojournalist does not recognize a bad image. A bad photograph will be remembered more than a good one simply because photo editors and directors view primarily good images daily, so the bad ones stand out.

HOW TO SHOOT PORTFOLIO SLIDES

Because most publications and photojournalism students who don't use digital cameras shoot with negative film instead of positive (or slide film) these images must be converted to create slide portfolios. There are many ways to get your work into slide form. The traditional method of shooting slides of prints is still an option if the technological tools are not available to have slides made from digital image files. Some professional labs will shoot the slides for you. However, when shooting copy slides of portfolio prints, there are many things to consider.

Matching Film with the Light Source

Most copy stands have two to four lights equidistant from the platform base. The angle of the lights can be adjusted; the best results are produced at a 45-degree angle from the base. Match the film to the light source. When using tungsten light (3200K), use tungsten slide film. The lower the ISO of the film, the sharper the image will appear. If tungsten slide film is not available, use daylight slide film and an 80A (blue) filter on the camera lens. If the light source is 3400K, use an 80B filter. Use an 82A filter if Type A film is used with a 3200K light source.

When a studio strobe light is used to shoot the slides, use daylight film. If there is a combination of black and white and color prints to copy, use color film to shoot all the prints. When color slides and processed black and white slides (see below) are placed together in a slide page, the differences in the color cast of the film base can make one or the other look washed out. Similarly, use the same type of film to shoot all the slides so that the look of the slides is consistent. For example, Kodak and Fuji films have different color masks on the film base. One appears warm-toned, the other cool.

Black and White Slides

Many portfolios will include a combination of black and white and color work. As was stated above, it is best to use the same color slide film to shoot the black and white prints that is used to shoot the color prints. However, Kodak has a reversal kit to make black and white slides using black and white negative film. Using T-Max 100 ISO film is recommended with this kit. The black and white slides that are processed with this kit have a warmer tone value than black and white slides copied with color slide film. This might be preferable if the entire portfolio is black and white.

Polarizing Filters

A polarizing filter can be used when shooting copy slides to increase the saturation. Polarizing filters for the copy stand lights can also be used to reduce reflections in the dark areas of glossy prints.

Lens Choice and Exposure

A normal-length macro lens will produce the best results. Zoom lenses with macro modes will usually produce slides that are not as sharp. Make sure the camera body is parallel to the prints. Determining the exposure is critical because slide film is being used. Use an 18% gray card when metering for the proper exposure. If filters are being used, do not forget to increase the exposure to compensate for the filter factor.

Masking Slides

If some prints are not proportionate to a 35mm film format, the slides can be masked with tape to eliminate the dead space in the frame. Most camera stores stock tape made especially for this purpose. Another alternative is to trim the borders off the prints and place black velvet or black paper under the print when shooting. However, because of the material and exposure, the backing might not look 100% black when the slide is projected.

Originals and Duplicates

After an original set of copy slides has been produced, have several sets of duplicates made by a professional lab. Keep the original set to produce more duplicates as needed in the future.

Labeling the Slides

Slide labels can be printed from most word-processing programs and look more professional than merely writing on the slide. If labels are not used, be sure to label all the portfolio slides consistently with the name, date, and title or subject in the same place for each slide. If entering the slides in a contest, check the contest rules. There are usually specific instructions for labeling slides. Although plastic slide pages are usually used for slide portfolio presentation, black cardboard slide holders enhance the presentation quality.

It is no longer necessary to place the copyright symbol on the work to copyright it. However, the Copyright Office advises doing so to ensure that all rights will be protected. Three things should be included: the copyright symbol or the word *copyright*, the date of the work, and your name. However, if a professional lab requests duplicates slides, you must give written permission for the lab to produce the duplicates (copyright is discussed further in Chapter 11.)

PRESENTATION AND GROUPING YOUR WORK TO PLAY TO ITS STRENGTHS

There are differing opinions among professionals concerning the presentation and grouping of portfolio images. The more feedback is solicited from professionals and teachers, the better. This will help to filter out weaker images and identify images that some viewers might have a subjective bias for or against. Soliciting feedback will also help the beginning photojournalist to recognize any personal strength or style that is emerging. It is important to begin the series of images (whether in a slide page or in a slide player program) with one of the strongest images and to end strongly as well. Many ways of grouping or putting the images together in a certain order are generally subjective and will vary from one viewer to the other. That's why it is important to get many people to view the work. If a common opinion begins to show up, follow that advice. However, be wary of different subject or compositional biases. The images do not have to be grouped in the categories of sports, features, news, and portraits. In fact, varying the categories can give a visual rhythm to the portfolio.

PREPARING DIGITAL FILES FOR SLIDE OUTPUT

Many professional labs are now equipped to output digital files to transparency film. The cost varies, as do the specifications for the image file. After locating a lab to do this, call and ask for specific instructions concerning file size, mode, and format. Figure 9.4 shows an example of specifications needed when scanning.

FIGURE 9.4

**Suggested Specifications
When Having Slides
Made from Digital
Image Files**

**SCAN NEGATIVE OR POSITIVE
(BLACK AND WHITE OR COLOR)**

Mode: RGB

File format: TIFF

Resolution: 200–300 dpi

Pixel amount: 8,192 longest dimension
6,553 other dimension

Save on Zip or Jaz disk

It is usually less expensive to have one original slide made from the digital file and then have duplicates made. This will vary depending on the lab prices and services offered.

RÉSUMÉ WITH COVER LETTER

The slide page portfolio, disk, or CD-ROM should always be accompanied by a résumé and cover letter. Even when dropping a slide sheet off for critique, always include a résumé.

A student résumé should consist of one page with an additional page for references. Never list references upon request on the résumé. When surveyed, many professionals stated that because of time constraints, it is preferable to have this information already listed. The résumé should include biographical information, education, work history, awards or honors, and references (see Figure 9.5).

FIGURE 9.5

**Example of Information to
Include on a Résumé**

Name

Address

Professional Experience:

Education:

Technology Proficiencies:
(for example, Photoshop, Quark, experience with digital cameras)

Honors/Awards:

References on next page (if this page is full).
Include names, titles, addresses, phone numbers, and e-mail addresses.
Include at least one from your educational background, one employer, and a successful contact in the field if you have one. Always contact these people and ask their permission to use them as references.

AREAS FOR DISCUSSION

■ Discuss tailoring a portfolio when applying to a specific publication. For example, a publication that emphasizes sports or the environment.

■ Discuss the factors of costs and access to professional labs versus shooting the portfolio slides the old-fashioned way.

■ Discuss the importance of having many peers, professionals, and educators view the portfolio before sending it out to apply for internships or jobs.

■ Discuss events such as the National Press Photographers Association short courses as a place to have your portfolio reviewed.

chapter 10

CD-ROM AND WEB SITE PORTFOLIOS

Various software program applications are used to put digital image files into a portfolio presentation. QuickShow, Hyper Slide Player, and PowerPoint are just a few of the programs used. Regardless of the software used, the images must be scanned for screen resolution and saved in the appropriate file format required by the software application, usually JPEG, GIF, or PICT. However, as software versions are updated, image file formats that are accepted for import may vary.

After the images are placed in the software application, the slide show portfolio can be saved on a Zip disk or a Jaz disk, burned onto a CD, and/or placed on the web. (See the website for this book to see an example of an on-line portfolio.) Caption information can be included in each image slide, or captions can be prepared as a separate slide at the beginning or end of the portfolio presentation (see Figure 10.1).

QuickShow is a shareware slide player application. Listed below are instructions to prepare images for this application. After the images have been

1. Use a multisession or rewritable blank CD.

2. Choose a software application to use for the digital image files, such as QuickShow or Hyper Slide Player.

3. Scan all portfolio slides or negatives at screen resolution (72 dpi) and at the appropriate size. (Prepare for the lowest common denominator of viewing so that images will not be cropped if viewed on a small screen—640 × 480 pixels for 15-inch screen viewing.) Alternatively, resize and change the resolution of existing digital image files.

4. Scan in RGB mode for screen viewing (including black and white negatives).

5. Save the image files in the appropriate file format (JPEG, GIF, or PICT).

6. Name each image file either alphabetically or numerically, depending on the slide player application.

7. Create a title slide with name, address, phone number, and e-mail information.

8. Create a caption slide, or (using Photoshop layers) paste the image file into a new Photoshop window large enough to include the caption underneath the image. (Instruction is provided later in this chapter.)

9. Save all image and text files in one portfolio file folder.

10. Using the software that comes with your CD-ROM writer, burn the portfolio file onto the CD. (Specific instructions for a program called Toaster are listed in this chapter.)

FIGURE 10.1

Suggested Specifications for Preparing a CD-ROM Portfolio

prepared, the QuickShow application icon is dragged onto the disk. Automatic compression is built into this application. A 2-megabyte, high-density disk can hold ten to fifteen color images scanned at the specifications listed below. However, using a Zip disk is recommended. The failure rate of Zip disks is much lower than that of ordinary floppy disks.

PREPARING PHOTOSHOP IMAGE FILES FOR QUICKSHOW

To prepare Photoshop image files for a QuickShow portfolio, do the following:

1. Scan negatives or slides, using the following specifications:
   - Size: 480 pixels × 640 pixels (maximum)
   - Resolution: 72 (screen resolution)
   - Mode: RGB (color or black and white)
2. Save as PICT or JPEG files.
3. Name the files alphabetically (e.g., cover slide: a, 1st image; b, etc.).
4. Save the files on a floppy, Zip, or Jaz disk that has the QuickShow application (see Figure 10.2).

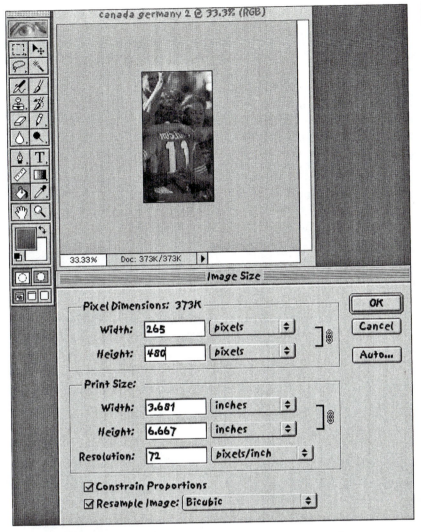

FIGURE 10.2

Resolution and Dimensions for Portfolio Slides to Be Viewed in a Digital Slide Application

Resolution should be 72, and pixel dimensions for the lowest common denominator screen should not exceed 640 × 480 pixels.

Photo by Vernon Bryant.

PREPARING SLIDES IN PHOTOSHOP FOR IMAGES WITH CAPTIONS

To make cover slides or slides for images and captions, do the following:

1. Open Photoshop.
2. Go to the File menu, and select New.
3. Set the image size to a height of 480 pixels and a width of 640 pixels. (Be sure the increments are set in pixels.)
4. Set the resolution to 72.
5. Set the mode to RGB.
6. For Contents, select Background Color or White (not Transparent).
7. Click OK. A blank window will appear.
8. Go to the Window menu, select Show Palettes, and select Show Swatches.
9. Click on a color. This color will appear as the background color in the tool menu. Black, white, or gray is recommended for a professional look that will not take away from the photographic image.
10. Click on the paint bucket, and then click in the screen. The screen will fill with the color.

To put the image in the slide window, do the following:

1. Open the image file in Photoshop. Make sure the image resolution is 72 and the size is smaller than 640 × 480 pixels to ensure that it will fit into the new slide area, leaving room for the caption information. Check this by going to the Image menu and selecting Image Size.
2. Select all, and copy the image.
3. Click on the newly created image window.
4. Paste the image into the new slide window.

Note: Photoshop will have created a new layer automatically as you paste the image into the window. When the slide is complete with text and image, flatten and merge layers before saving the slide. To do this, go to the Window menu and select Show Layers. Toggle down by clicking and holding on the right area from the Layers menu box to flatten and merge.

To put text in your slide, do the following:

1. Click in the text tool (T) and click in the open screen window.
2. Choose the font, color, and point size for the text.
3. Make sure antialiased is checked.
4. Type the caption or title slide information. (Remember to put in "returns" where necessary for text placement. Once the text has been placed in the window, spacing cannot be changed.)
5. Click OK, and the text will appear in the window.
6. Use the move tool (top right) to position the text.
7. Flatten and merge all layers before saving.
8. Save the file as JPEG or PICT.

See Figures 10.3 and 10.4 for examples of slides in Photoshop and QuickShow.

FIGURE 10.3

Slide with Cutline Added

This photo can be placed in a Photoshop slide area, and the cutline can be placed underneath the image.

Photo by Vernon Bryant.

Joy Ray, mother of three, prays in front of Wedgwood Baptist Church in Fort Worth. She says the shooting victims could easily have been her children.

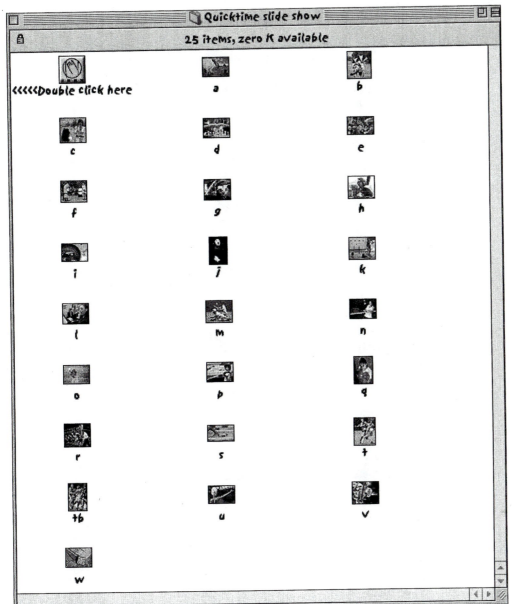

FIGURE 10.4

QuickTime Slide Show

This screen shows a view of thumbnail images placed in a file folder with a digital slide playing application.

Photos by Vernon Bryant.

BURNING FILES ONTO A CD

After the image files are placed in a file folder with a slide player application, the portfolio can be burned (written) onto a CD. Most CD-ROM writers come with the software necessary to write to CDs.

Before burning a CD, check the following:

- Is the computer reading the CD burner?
- Is the format the files are going to be copied in ISO 9660? (This can be read on a Mac or PC.)
- Are the image files all in one folder on the computer desktop?

To burn a CD using the Toast program, do the following:

1. Start the Program.
2. Click on the Data button. A new dialog box will be shown. At the bottom of this dialog box are three other buttons.
3. Click the New CD button. In the window above, a CD icon should appear. It should be called Untitled_CD. Clicking twice on the CD icon will let you change the name of the CD. (Note: you will be unable to change the name of the CD after burning.)
4. When you are ready to put files on the CD, click on the Add button.
5. Find the folders or files you want and place the files onto the CD by clicking on the Add button.
6. When you are finished selecting the files to add to the CD, click on the Done button at the bottom right of the dialog box. This takes you back to the first window.
7. Click on the Write CD button.
8. In the dialogue box, select Write Session. This will allow you to add files on the CD. The Write Disk selection will permanently lock the disk, and you will be unable to add more files.
9. Once you have made a selection, the CD will begin to be written. Do not move or shake the table or the CD burner.
10. When the CD burner is finished, a dialogue box will appear and ask whether you would like to verify or cancel. Select none of these options. The dialogue box will disappear, and the computer will automatically verify that the files are on the disk.
11. When the computer is finished verifying, it will ask you to eject the CD.

CREATING A PORTFOLIO WEB SITE

Simplicity should be a major factor in creating a portfolio web site. Small image files and logical navigation should also be considered. When a potential client or employer visits the site, the visual information should download quickly. Figure 10.5 outlines the first steps in creating a portfolio web site.

Web site designer Jon Freilich says that one of the biggest mistakes is to start an ambitious project and put it online half completed. He recommends starting with a small, simple web site that is designed to grow. Create a design that uses small photographs with just a few per page to minimize downloading time (see Figures 10.6 and 10.7). Freilich also recommends using a simple way to navigate the site. He explains that if your site navigation is confusing, it will tend to drive people away.

FIGURE 10.5

Brief Outline for Creating a Portfolio Web Site

1. Select a web-authoring program such as Dreamweaver, Frontpage, or Composer or use HTML formatting.
2. Scan all images for screen resolution and place titled images in a file folder. (This is important because once image files are imported into the web page, a link is created to the image file. If the image is moved, the image will not appear on the web page.)
3. Keep image size small for easy downloading and viewing.
4. Decide on background and text colors.
5. Create a layout template that provides logical navigation throughout the site.

FIGURE 10.6

Professional Portfolio Web Page

Each category reveals a different image.

Photo by Joe Stefanchik. Web site designed by Jon Freilich.

FIGURE 10.7

Different Images Appear as the Viewer Scrolls through the Image Categories

Photo by Joe Stefanchik. Web site designed by Jon Freilich.

Basic Design Theory

Basic design and color theory should be considered in creating a portfolio web site. Even though the monitor screen is a two-dimensional surface, the navigational ability of web space gives the illusion of a three-dimensional space. Therefore, attention to both two- and three-dimensional design will help to render a well-designed space.

Design elements are as follows:

Form

Line

Texture (or simulated texture)

Color

Space

Light (in some media)

The following are some important design principles:

Continuity

Rhythm: repetition, alternation, and progression

Emphasis

Balance: asymmetry versus symmetry

Variety

Structuring or use of design elements makes it possible to achieve one or more design principles. In any medium (including web page design), not all of the elements and principles will always be used. For example, designing a web site might employ only the use of color, space, and movement (or navigation) throughout the site. Moving through a web space is analogous to moving through a building or letting your eyes wander through sculpture. Sketch your design on paper, but create a three-dimensional space similar to an architect's blueprint.

Basic Color Theory

White light primaries (or additive primary colors) are different from pigment primary colors. Primary colors and their complements are as follows:

Pigment	White Light
red–green	red–cyan
yellow–violet	green–magenta
blue–orange	blue–yellow

Although the body of research on online screen page design and use of color in online pages is still evolving, basic color and design theory can be applied. Complementary colors will intensify each other when used together. Values such as black, white, and gray can be used to isolate or outline other colors in text, graphics, or photographic images. Gray is always a good choice as a background for color photographic images. The visual perception of the gray area will shift to the dominant color's complement, therefore intensifying the dominant color and adding a three-dimensional quality to the screen page.

Various software applications can be used to create web pages. Instruction is provided below for Dreamweaver, a Macromedia web authoring application that is compatible with Director, Flash, and other Macromedia programs. If using Photoshop to prepare your images for a web site is not an option, many web page programs have an imaging or photo editor within the application. These image editors provide tools to crop, resize, and make adjustments to image files.

FIGURE 10.8

Define Sites Menu Box

Creating a Web Page in Dreamweaver

To begin creating a web page using Dreamweaver, follow these steps:

1. Create a new file folder. (Do this before you open Dreamweaver.) This will be your *root folder*. It is best to put all the images you will bring into the page into this root folder before you insert the images into the web page. Name this root folder the same name you intend to name the site.
2. Open Dreamweaver.
3. If the box in Figure 10.8 appears, click on Define Sites. If this box does not appear, go to the Site menu, select Define Sites, and this box will appear (see Figure 10.9).
4. Click on New. The box in Figure 10.10 will appear.

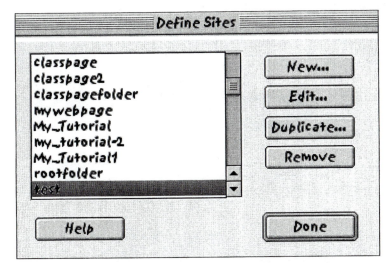

FIGURE 10.9

Menu Box to Define New Site

FIGURE 10.10

Menu Box for Site Name and Root Folder

FIGURE 10.11

Menu Box to Select
Local Root Folder

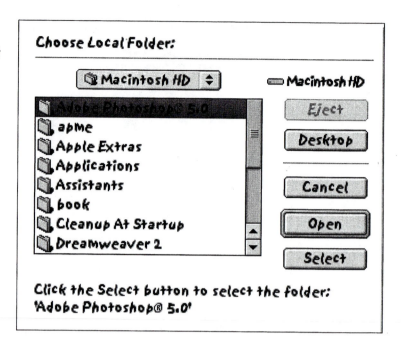

5. Name the site the same name that you named your root folder. In the local root folder blank, click on the folder to the right. The box in Figure 10.11 will appear.
6. Direct the menu to the root folder you created, click on Select, and this box will indicate your changes (see Figure 10.12).
7. Note that Local Info is highlighted. If you were going to FTP the page, this is where you would set the information for where to send it.
8. Click on OK. The window in Figure 10.13 will appear.

FIGURE 10.12

Menu Box to Set
Site as Local or
to Enter URL

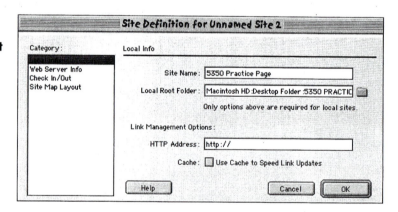

FIGURE 10.13

Cache File Option

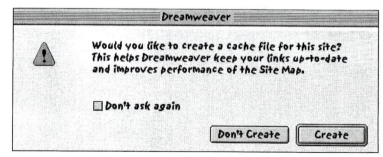

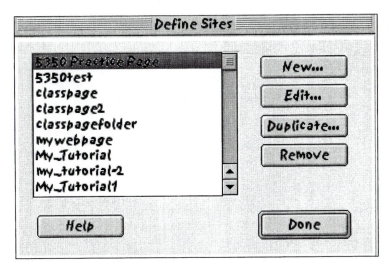

FIGURE 10.14

**Correct Root
Folder Should
Be Highlighted**

9. For class use, click on Don't Create. The window in Figure 10.14 will then appear.
10. Make sure your root folder is the one that is highlighted, and click on Done.
11. Save the page to the root folder and title the page *Index.html*.
12. Go to the Modify menu and select Page Properties. Set the background color, using the eyedropper. Also set the text and links.

To import an image into the Dreamweaver web page, do the following:

1. Go to the Insert menu and select Image (see Figure 10.15).
2. A dialogue box will direct you to select the image from file.

Insert	Modify	Text	Commands	Site	
Image			Option ⌘I		
Table			Option ⌘T		
Horizontal Rule					
Layer					
Applet					
ActiveX					
Plugin					
Flash			Option ⌘F		
Shockwave			Option ⌘D		
Rollover Image					
Form					
Form Object			▶		
Named Anchor			Option ⌘A		
Comment					
Script					
Line Break			Shift Return		
Non-Breaking Space			Option Space		
Server-Side Include					
Head			▶		

FIGURE 10.15

Insert Menu Options

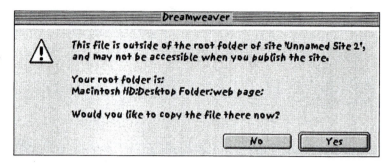

FIGURE 10.16

**Reminder to Copy
Image to Root Folder**

> **Dreamweaver**
>
> ⚠ This file is outside of the root folder of site 'Unnamed Site 2', and may not be accessible when you publish the site.
>
> Your root folder is:
> Macintosh HD:Desktop Folder:web page:
>
> Would you like to copy the file there now?
>
> [No] [Yes]

3. Dreamweaver will automatically prompt you to copy the image to your root folder if the image has not already been placed there (see Figure 10.16). However, as was stated above, it is always best to have all the image files placed in your web page folder before building the page, no matter what software application is being used.
4. The image will be imported into the page. The image can be spaced on the page or dragged into a newly created layer.

Adding bells and whistles to a portfolio page is not recommended. The prospective employer wants to see the portfolio images without distractions. It is a good idea to put the images on a grid similar to that on a slide page and have each smaller image link to a larger version. Alternatively, position your strongest image in each category on the index page and link it to specific category pages with the remaining image. There should be a résumé link as well. Although many professionals voice a subjective bias against animation, some portfolio pages use text animation on the index page of the title or name. Listed below are simple instructions on how to animate information in Dreamweaver.

To create animated text or image, do the following:

1. Go to the Window menu and select Timeline to make sure the Timeline box is open.
2. Go to Insert Layer (an image or text must be placed in a layer to animate).
3. Go to the side menu and click on the Insert Image button to add an image. Alternatively, place text in the layer.
4. Go to the Modify menu and select Add Object to Timeline.
5. In the Timeline box, click on the Keyframe at the end of the highlighted bar.
6. Now click and drag the layer by clicking in the layer until you see a hand appear at the top left of the layer. Click and drag the layer where you want the animation to end. Save the file.
7. Hold down the play button to see the animation.
8. Go to File Preview in Browser to see the animation.

AREAS FOR DISCUSSION

- Call newspapers and magazines and ask photo directors what format they prefer to receive portfolios.
- Discuss the various ways of arranging portfolio images to play to the strength of each image.
- Discuss the pros and cons of combining black and white images with color images in a portfolio.

chapter **11**

COPYRIGHT ISSUES

Digital technology and new tools have created new questions regarding copyright issues and fair use. Not only has the ability to alter images become easier, but also the ability to take images directly from online publications simplifies the act of copyright infringement. In addition, as the repurposing, or reuse, of photographs for various media formats—traditional print, video broadcast, and online—becomes commonplace among news organizations, issues regarding image rights and licenses are becoming a major concern in employing freelance photojournalists.

This chapter gives a summary of copyright law as it is currently shaped since changes made in 1988 and in relation to the 1998 Digital Millennium Copyright Act. Specific areas such as registration and rights are outlined. Consult the book web site for updates.

COPYRIGHT LAW

Copyright law falls under the larger umbrella of intellectual property law. This area of law also governs trademarks, patents, and unfair competition. The first federal copyright act was enacted in 1790. It has been revised and amended several times, most notably in 1909, 1976, and 1988. The Digital Millennium Copyright Act, discussed later in the chapter, was passed by Congress in 1998 and expands the Telecommunications Act.

WHAT IS PROTECTED AND FOR HOW LONG

The facts of news cannot be copyrighted. However, the description and style of presentation of the news are protected as soon as they are in a fixed form. A televised news program, an entire edition of a newspaper, and a news web site are examples of a particular style of presentation of the news that is protected by copyright owned by that news organization (see Figure 11.1).

FIGURE 11.1

The Entire Online Content Package Is Copyright Protected

Pilotonline.com, *The Virginian-Pilot.*

MILITARY

News / Business / Sports / U.S.& World / Opinion / Classifieds / Weather

AP Military
USS Wisconsin
Recent stories
Pilot archives
TalkNet
Military boards
Ships
Squadrons
Ship tracking
Nassau
Saipan
Truman
G. Washington
Web links
The Flagship
U.S. Navy
National sites
Local sites
Status of Navy
E-mail a sailor
MARSgrams
Contact us
Military reporters

e-mail this story - get news by e-mail

January 11, 2001

Photos: The LST-325 arrives

By STEVE EARLEY, STAFF PHOTOGRAPHER
© 2001, The Virginian-Pilot

Background coverage: WWII ship and aged crew cheered at Alabama arrival

LST-325 crew member Jack Carter listens to questions from children as the ship docks in Mobile, Ala, on Wednesday.

Included within that style of presentation of the news are the news photographs. All photographs made by the photojournalists working for the news organization and by freelance photojournalists are published within that specific style of presentation of the news. As such, these images may be fully owned and copyrighted by the news organization as works made under a work-for-hire situation (discussed later in the chapter) or images that have been licensed for a specific use from the freelancer. In this case the freelancer retains the copyright for the individual photograph.

The creator of a photograph owns the copyright of the photograph when it is not made as part of a work-for-hire agreement, which establishes the employer as the creator. A work-for-hire photograph is protected for 95 years from the year of creation. When not work-for-hire, a photograph is copyright protected for the photographer's life plus 70 years.

Publication of a photograph is not a requirement for copyright protection. The expansion of copyright protection to cover unpublished work was one of the major changes resulting from the 1976 Copyright Act. Copyright protection begins as soon as the photograph is in a fixed form. An unpublished work-for-hire photograph is protected for 120 years. This length of time is a 20-year extension added by Congress in 1998 and applies retroactively to works created after January 1, 1978, in addition to new and current work.

WHOSE WORK IS WHOSE?

Work for Hire

When working as a photojournalist for a news organization the term *work-for-hire* means that the employer owns the copyright to all of the photographs taken within the scope of that employment. This is standard unless other terms are agreed upon in writing. However, if the photographer takes photographs under his or her own initiative and expense, in no relation to his or her professional work, and not as part of the employment relationship, then the photographer owns the copyright for these images.

Freelance

The court views freelance contributors as independent contractors. Unless there is a specific contractual agreement that states otherwise, when a freelancer creates a work such as a photograph, the freelancer owns the copyright and the work is his or her intellectual property. Generally, the freelancer then agrees on the number of times the image is to be used. In the past, a standard freelance contract usually secured, at minimum, first-use, one-time rights to all the images resulting from the shooting assignment. However, contractual agreements between news organizations and photographers are changing, and this is affecting the state of freelance photojournalism; as a result, copyright ownership is changing.

As was stated previously in the chapter, with most news organizations now repurposing visual and text content for the web, many freelance contracts have been modified to cover a variety of rights and licenses. Now (owing primarily to the repurposing of content), most news organizations try to secure all rights for current and future use for all media for the assignment covered, therefore owning the copyright (see the case studies in Chapter 12). In 1998 a federal court ruled in favor of the Associated Press in a lawsuit between AP and the National Association of Freelance Photographers. (The NAFP was formed to protect copyright ownership by freelancers.) The court ruled that AP has legal claim to copyright for all pictures taken for it by freelancers on assignment (see Chapter 12). However, different news organizations handle this differently, and contracts can vary depending on the photographer and the assignment.

UNFAIR COMPETITION

Another issue that arises as images are repurposed for a variety of media publishing formats is the question of unfair competition. Because most newspapers have online news publications in addition to the traditional print edition, online content (both visual and text) is now competing in a broader market. Newspapers that generally would not be considered direct competitors because they serve different markets are now competing online.

Unfair competition is a legal concept that has been used as a supplement to copyright law. In contrast to copyright law, which is a federal statutory law, unfair competition is a tort action that has developed as a result of state court decisions. The legal definition of unfair competition (sometimes referred to as misappropriation) prevents one news content provider from pirating content from another.

Work-for-hire photojournalists who might in the past have taken on freelance assignments for noncompetitors are now limited to a smaller venue if the rights to those images are signed over for web publication. This also limits the market for freelance photojournalists in regard to "gentlemen's agreements" about not working for direct competitors.

COPYRIGHT VERSUS PUBLIC DOMAIN

If the author, photographer, or owner of the work chooses not to claim copyright protection, the works falls into the public domain and is considered to belong to everyone. Anyone may reproduce a work that is in the public domain. Images taken by the Farm Security Administration are now in the public domain. These images are available on several web sites. The original images are housed within the Library of Congress (see Figure 11.2).

However, if copyright protection is claimed, the owner of the copyright has the exclusive right to take the following actions:

- Reproduce the copyrighted material
- Create derivative works
- Distribute copies
- Perform or display the work
- Allow others to use the work under specified conditions

COPYRIGHT AND NOTICE

A photograph or a style of news presentation such as a newspaper edition (as discussed earlier in the chapter) is under copyright protection the moment it is created in a fixed form. Inserting the copyright notice is no longer necessary. However, if a notice is inserted, three elements should be included:

- The copyright symbol, the word *copyright*, or the abbreviation *copr*
- The year of the first publication or creation of the work
- The name of the owner of the copyright

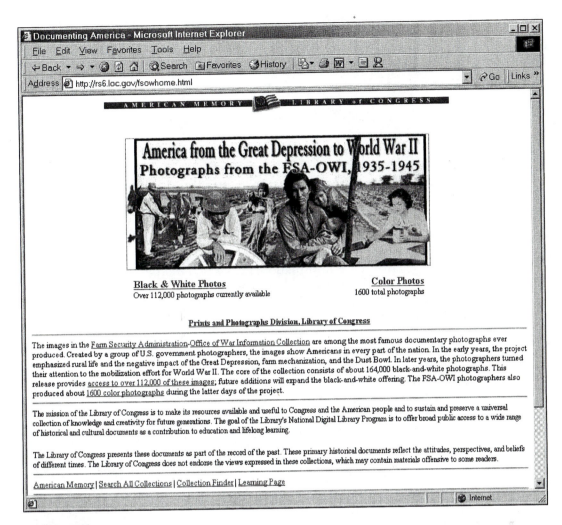

FIGURE 11.2

Farm Security Administration Web Site from the Library of Congress

The Library of Congress, lcweb2.loc.gov/fsowhome.html

COPYRIGHT REGISTRATION FOR PUBLISHED OR UNPUBLISHED WORK

Registration is not a condition of copyright protection. Copyright registration is a legal formality that is intended to make a public record of the basic facts of a particular copyright. It provides several advantages if an infringement suit is filed.

To register a copyright, do the following:

- Obtain the forms from the U.S. Copyright Office, Library of Congress, Washington, DC 20559. For serial publications—newspapers, magazines, and the like—use Form SE. For visual arts work, use Form VA.
- Pay the subscribed fee.
- Mail the completed form, the fee, and two copies of the work to the Copyright office.

A collection of photographs can be registered with as few as two photographs and no maximum limit if the following conditions are met:

- The elements are assembled in an orderly form.
- The combined elements bear a single title identifying the collection as a whole.
- The copyright claimant in all of the elements and in the collection as a whole is the same.
- All of the elements are by the same author, or, if they are by different authors, at least one of the authors has contributed copyrightable authorship to each of the elements.
- Note: A single registration may also be made for all the copyrightable elements in a single unit of publication if the copyright claimant is the same for all elements.

As of July 1, 1999, the basic fee was $30. Check the web site for this book for updates regarding fee information. Fees will differ when multiple copies of a serial publication are registered. Registering either before an infringement occurs or within 90 days of publication provides more legal remedies if a case of infringement is taken to court. Registration must be done before an infringer is sued.

Registration may be made at any time within the life of the copyright. Since passage of the 1978 law, an unpublished work that is registered does not have to be registered again on publication, although the copyright owner may register the published edition.

By registering the copyright, the owner establishes a public record of the copyright claim. Registration is necessary before an infringement suit may be filed in court for works of U.S. origin and for foreign works not originating in a Berne Union country. (The Berne Union, established in 1934 by France, Italy, Spain, and the UK, works for international acceptance of sound principles of foreign investment insurance and export credit insurance.) If done before or within five years of publication, registration will establish prima facie evidence in court of the validity of the copyright. If registration is done within three months after publication of the work or before an infringement of the work, statutory damages and attorney's fees will be available to the copyright owner in court actions. Otherwise, only an award of actual damages and profits is available to the copyright owner. Registration allows the owner of the copyright to record the registration with the U.S. Customs Service for protection against the importation of infringing copies.

WHAT IS INFRINGEMENT?

Copyright infringement is the unauthorized use of a copyrighted image. Infringement can be as blatant as the taking of an image from an online publication for use in another without getting permission or as subtle as creating a drawing based on a photograph that contains all the subtleties of the original. Copyright law is civil law, not criminal law, so if infringement occurs, a person can be sued, not charged with a crime.

FAIR USE

When use of a work is taken to court as a copyright infringement case, one of the most common defenses is fair use. The fair use doctrine is an attempt by the courts to balance the copyright owner's right to compensation with the public's interest. The 1976 Copyright Act established guidelines for determining fair use. To qualify as fair use of a copyrighted image when it is used without permission, the following factors must be considered for defense of that use:

- The purpose and character of the use, including whether the use is commercial or for nonprofit educational purposes
- The nature of the copyrighted work
- The percentage and substantiality of the total work used
- The effect of the use on the potential market for or value of the copyrighted work

Fair use also protects the unauthorized use of copyrighted photographs when the images contribute to the public's understanding of an important event, usually a breaking news situation. Most notably, in *Time Inc.* v. *Bernard Geis Associates*, drawings based on photographs of the Kennedy assassination were used without permission granted from the copyright owner of the photographs. The court found that even though this constituted copyright infringement, the public interest outweighed the unauthorized use.

Another area in which fair use is being challenged lies in the reselling of images from sporting events. Some sports franchises give press credentials based on agreements of restricted use of the images from the event. Most franchises take the position that use of the photographs of the game should be limited to the dissemination of news.

Although the news organization owns the copyright for the photographs, many people believe that reselling the images is not fair use because it is not part of the news dissemination of the game that was photographed. However, the opposing argument sees the reselling as fair use because the news organization owns the copyright for the images (see the case *NBA* v. *The New York Times* in Chapter 12).

Fair use also includes public access to copyrighted images when provided for under the Federal Freedom of Information Act. When photographs are part of a federal agency's records, the photographs may be inspected or photocopied. In addition to fair use, another defense that has been used is that the use for satire or parody, which falls under freedom of expression. However, this use is not always protected.

COPYRIGHT AND INTERNATIONAL ISSUES

There is not an international copyright that will automatically protect a work throughout the entire world. Protection against unauthorized use in another country depends on the laws of that country. Most countries do offer protection to foreign works under certain conditions that have been organized through international copyright treaties and conventions such as the Berne Convention, the world's primary international copyright agreement, which was established in 1886. Although not a participant in the Berne Convention, the United States has participated in the Universal Copyright Convention and has also entered into reciprocal agreements with many countries.

THE DIGITAL MILLENNIUM COPYRIGHT ACT

The Digital Millennium Copyright Act, passed in 1998, sets up a notice-and-take-down process by which potential plaintiffs tell an Internet service provider (ISP) when their copyrighted property is being infringed on by a web site hosted by the ISP. After the ISP finds out whether the material is actually a copyright infringement, it is allowed 10 days before being considered a copyright infringer. This enables copyright owners to shut down web sites without going to court. ISPs are exempt from copyright liability if they act as copyright enforcers (see the David McCreery case in Chapter 12).

WHY COPYRIGHT ISSUES ARE CHANGING

Recently the Supreme Court handed down a decision that, if not reversed, will greatly affect freelance work published on the web, specifically archived databases. The court decided that publishers cannot include the individual work of freelance contributors in electronic databases without the freelancer's permission (see the Tasini case in Chapter 12).

In addition to specifying use in databases and archives, publishers must now specifically provide for the license of online rights in their freelance agreements. This decision has the potential to affect magazines and newspapers originally published in print that have already been transferred to online archives. Under the Supreme Court decision the publisher's electronic reproduction of a freelancer's photograph or article that has not been licensed for such rights may infringe on the freelancer's copyright, even if the work was originally published years ago.

PHOTOGRAPHS IN ONLINE NEWS PUBLICATIONS

The emerging industry standard is to use software to watermark the photographs. Currently, a majority of newspapers are using Digimarc as a plug-in with Photoshop to mark and track images. Essentially, by using software to track the watermarks, Digimarc can locate examples of the photographs being used throughout the web. Depending on the level of copyright infringement, newspapers can then decide whether or not to pursue legal remedies against the unauthorized use.

Although online photographs are low-resolution images and small, the availability and ease of taking this visual content will continue to make this an issue. Until recently, it was possible to hold online service providers strictly liable for the infringing actions of their users. However, with the recent passage of the Digital Millennium Copyright Act, Congress provided an exemption for Internet service providers that are innocently unaware of infringing activity.

Other avenues are being explored. An online pilot project conducted by iCopyright.com was created to provide for automated copyright permissions and reprints. Although most of the publishers involved in the program are from the technology trade, several newspaper publishers have joined the pilot program, including Washingtonpost-Newsweek Interactive, the new-media division of the *Washington Post*. The program allows for instant reuse or reprint of content from registered publishers, and the publishers choose which options they want to give customers. Options offered include everything from e-mailed articles to glossy photographic reprints. The publisher sets the price for each of these services, or the publisher can choose to offer the content for free. There is no charge for a publisher to register for this service. The publisher pays when a customer purchases content for reuse. The irony is that the content (including photographs) is not watermarked or encrypted. This service relies on the honor system.

AREAS FOR DISCUSSION

- Discuss the changes that are occurring involving licensing rights for image use because news organizations are now publishing online in addition to traditional print.

- Contact a copyright attorney concerning gray areas that might arise when working as a freelance photojournalist.

chapter 12

CASE STUDIES AND ETHICS

Most cases of alleged copyright infringement of online news content have involved text, not pictures. However, the same issues and concerns involving online articles can be applied to photographs and images published online. Other copyright issues that are occurring with the advent of online news publications deal with the rights to reuse the images for the online media format and problems that may occur when those images are provided in online photo galleries for resale.

Because online photographs are low-resolution images, news organizations see the chance that they will be taken and reused in other traditional print publications as unlikely. However, as technology continues to evolve and screen resolution improves, this will not always be the case. Even though images from web sites are not showing up in other print publications, news photographs have been removed and used in other online publications.

As was mentioned in Chapter 11, many newspapers use the Digimarc Photoshop plug-in to watermark photographs within the web site. However, some newspapers rely solely on the overall copyright symbol posted for the entire web site as a preventive measure. Surprisingly, some newspapers have not had news photographs taken from the site but have had some minor problems with web advertising designs and banner ads being taken.

FAIR USE

Most copyright cases deal with misunderstanding of what constitutes fair use as a defense or publishing online without having previously negotiated for those rights. A particular case of copyright infringement is an indication of what may come to be in the new era of cyber copyright law.

Los Angeles Times v. The Free Republic

In the case of *Los Angeles Times* v. *The Free Republic,* stories were being cut and pasted from the online editions of the *L.A. Times* and the *Washington Post* into the *Free Republic* web site. The *Free Republic's* web site creators saw these postings as presentations for forums of discussions and, as such, fair use within copyright law. However, the same stories cost about $1.50 each from the *Times* and the *Post.* In addition to using fair use as a defense, the *Free Republic* also claimed the First Amendment right of freedom of expression for the site's commentators.

The federal court ruled in favor of the plaintiffs and against the fair use and First Amendment freedom of expression defenses. Because the articles were copied verbatim on a daily basis, the court saw this as more than was necessary to foster the solicited criticism of the way the media covers stories. In fact, most of the commentary on the site critiqued the stories and not how the stories were covered. Although this case did not involve the unauthorized use of photographs, online visual content can be taken and reused in much the same way.

Playboy Enterprises v. Sanfilippo

The bulk of cyber copyright infringement cases have dealt with the pirating of music over the Internet. However, when photographs are involved, *Playboy* has been the leader in the industry, pursuing a number of cases involving copyright infringement and photographs. These cases involve the web site owner or creator posting images owned by *Playboy.* In a 1988 case, *Playboy Enterprises* v. *Sanfilippo,* the site allegedly distributed 7,475 images owned by *Playboy. Playboy* won $3.74 million in statutory damages, at that time the largest damage award in the history of U.S. copyright law.

NBA v. The New York Times

In a lawsuit brought against the *New York Times,* the National Basketball Association (NBA) claimed that the *Times* violated a press credential restriction when it provided photographs from the 1999 NBA playoffs for sale as part of an online promotion. Five photographs from the playoffs were for sale in the NYT Store on the *Times'* web site. The suit, filed in July 2000 in New York State Supreme Court, dealt specifically with an NBA agreement with the *Times* regarding press credentials and the agreement of limited use of the photographs to news coverage of the games.

Some newspaper attorneys viewed this not only as fair use but also as a First Amendment right, especially in relation to the function of newspaper photo archives. In general, what makes this case problematic is the agreement, if any, of limited use between sports agencies or franchises and news organizations and the rights secured by copyright ownership of photographic news coverage. Initially, there was a limited opinion based on contract that did not defeat copyright claims. The *New York Times* reached a marketing settlement with the NBA and will be able to continue to sell photographs of NBA games through its online store. The agreement states that the *Times* will provide a direct web link from the newspaper's online store to nba.com, and the *Times* will feature the nba.com logo on NYTimes.com and in print advertisement that promotes the sale of *Times* photographs of the NBA games. What remains to be seen is how this settlement will affect sports coverage by newspapers and the resulting editorial use of the photographs in both traditional print and on the web.

COPYRIGHT INFRINGEMENT AND FREELANCERS

A number of controversies that are arising involving online photojournalism deal with freelancers and work being reused, or repurposed, on web sites of traditional print publications without those rights being negotiated or clearly stated in contracts. (This is discussed in Chapter 11.)

East Lansing Police Site

One repurposing situation involving the use of photojournalism on a web site was seen as a potential copyright infringement issue when photographs taken by a freelance photographer were posted on a site without his permission. East Lansing police posted several photographs, which had been taken during a riot, and asked for help in identifying the people in the photographs. Some of the riot pictures posted were taken by freelance photographer David Mc-Creery and had been confiscated by police with a search warrant from a store in East Lansing. The photos were published online without the consent of Mc-Creery, who held the copyright. The photographs were removed from the site after McCreery's attorney sent a letter of demand to the city to remove the photos. The attorney also sent a letter to the ISP that hosted the police site, putting it on notice that its hosting of the photographs constituted potential copyright infringement under the recently passed Digital Millennium Copyright Act. Figure 12.1 shows a screenshot of the police site that includes McCreery's photographs. Ironically, this screenshot is now in the public domain.

AP

As the number of newspaper web sites increases, the Associated Press changed the way it handled freelance contracts to provide for more secured rights, causing a wave of discontent throughout the freelance industry. This was the first measure, which has since become more common, of a news organization to negotiate for total copyright ownership from a freelance assignment.

A suit against AP, filed in 1996 by the National Association of Freelance Photographers (NAFP), an organization formed specifically for this case, included charges of antitrust, monopoly, and restraint of trade in relation to copyright ownership.

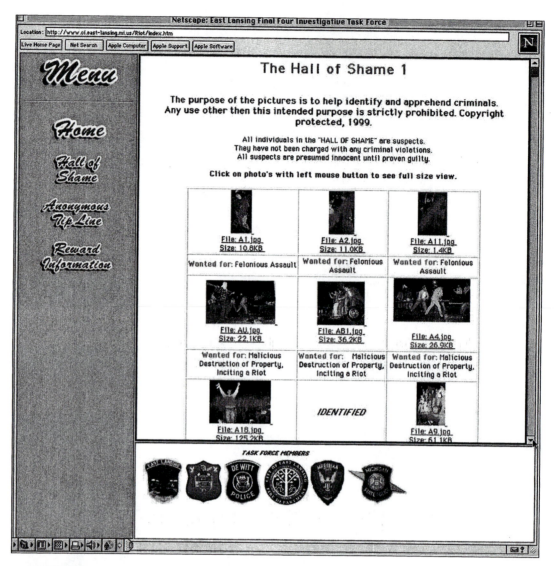

Screenshot of the Web Site That Used McCreery's Photographs

East Lansing Police Department's Web Page.

The court ruled that NAFP lacked standing as a professional organization to pursue the issue because the facts for each photographer would vary. The judge held that facts should be provided by individual plaintiffs on a case-by-case basis. NAFP opposed the transfer of copyright by freelancers to AP. As a result of this decision, many organizations, including the National Press Photographers Association, passed resolutions opposing this type of contractual agreement for freelancers.

Tasini v. *The New York Times*

Although the East Lansing police web site situation raises many questions involving the use and publication of photographs online that have yet to make it to court, the New York case mentioned in Chapter 11 might have a far-reaching affect because it is a binding decision.

A group of freelance writers, led by Jonathan Tasini, then president of the National Writers Union, won an eight-year copyright battle in June 2001 that is affecting the way freelance material (in this case, writing) can be archived and stored in databases. In this landmark decision, the U.S. Supreme Court ruled in agreement with the Second Circuit Court of Appeals, which had reversed the U.S. District Court decision. The Supreme Court found that the defendants, which included corporations that own major newspapers and magazines, were infringing on the copyrights of the plaintiffs by including their work in electronic databases without the writers' permission. In the 7–2 decision, the U.S. Supreme court ruled that publishers violated copyright law by posting freelance articles in electronic archives and by selling articles to database companies because the databases and archives were not seen as part of the collected work. The interpretation of what constitutes a "revision" of the collected works was critical to the court's ruling. A prior ruling in the district court had interpreted the inclusion of the collected works in electronic databases as a revision of the original work, and thereby exempt from copyright infringement. However, in agreement with the federal appeals court, the Supreme Court defined "revision" more narrowly. The Supreme Court Decision, written by Justice Ruth Bader Ginsberg, said online databases are different from microfilm archives and bound volumes because the databases present articles individually, not embedded in the context of a collection such as a traditional print publication. By placing the articles in the online databases, they are presented to and retrievable by the user in isolation, clear of the context of the original print publication. The impact could be great because of the archiving of newspapers, magazines, and database companies prior to the practice of covering those rights in contracts with freelancers. The *New York Times* began pulling freelance articles from its web-accessible archives and the ruling prompted other media companies to review their archives.

As was discussed in Chapter 11, most freelance contracts now state clearly whether the work is going to be used or repurposed for other forms of publications. Several papers commented that this decision would not affect their use of freelancers because most have been signing contracts granting electronic archiving rights since the mid-1990s. It remains to be seen how many people will make claims. However, on the basis of this Supreme Court decision, freelance work that was done without this agreement cannot be included in electronic databases or archives without the freelancer's permission.

Only those who have registered their work for copyright will be eligible for damages. The case was sent back to the lower courts to decide penalties. Tasini called for negotiations toward a settlement and a licensing system. The Times Co. said it would ask Congress to rewrite copyright law to reverse the effect. Although this case clearly affects articles, the overall issue could be applied to photographs supplied by freelance photojournalists as well.

MORE CONCERNING FREELANCERS

A class action lawsuit was filed in June 2000 on behalf of 1,000 freelancers seeking an injunction against the *Boston Globe*. The *Globe* was accused of attempting to coerce writers, illustrators, and photographers into signing an unfair contract demanding all rights in all media to past, present, and future creative works by freelance contributors. Allegedly the *Globe* told the freelancers that they would not be hired again unless they agreed to the conditions of the contract. The lawsuit, supported by local chapters of the National

Writers Union, the Graphic Artists Guild, and American Society of Media Photographers, charged the *Globe* with unfair and deceptive trade practices. (Consult the book web site for current information.)

PROTECTING PHOTOGRAPHS PUBLISHED ONLINE

In studies looking at this issue, most news organizations were not concerned with the limited amount of unauthorized use of photographs taken from the online news sites. The overall consensus is that, because they are low-resolution images, the photographs can be used again only online or as a poor-quality reproduction in print. As has been stated many times in this text, this may change as technology improves. In addition, as new sites are being created, such as the *Free Republic*, newspapers should revisit this issue.

As online sites increase, so will the need for newspapers to be concerned with copyright infringement. The nature of a news web site makes the material more accessible and the nature of web publishing creates a situation in which newspapers have to police the Internet themselves. Although the Internet is vast, even a minor attempt to secure copyright protection of photographs within online news sites will benefit news publications as more partnering sites continue to be created.

ETHICS IN THE AGE OF DIGITAL PHOTOGRAPHY

By John Long, Ethics Co-Chair and Past President of the NPPA

Two disclaimers are in order here:

- There are no hard and fast answers. The ethical standards that each person arrives at will be based on his or her cultural background and the principles on which his or her life is based.
- The advent of computers and digital photography has not created need for a whole new set of ethical standards. We merely have a new way of processing images, and the same principles that have guided us in traditional photojournalism should be the principles that guide us in the use of the computers.

We have many problems in journalism today that threaten our profession and in fact threaten the Constitution of the United States. Photo opportunities, lack of access to news events, rock show contracts, yellow tape, and bean counters are just a few. Everyone has a spin; everyone wants to control the news media.

The major problem that we face as photojournalists is the fact that the public is losing faith in us. They no longer believe everything they see. All images are called into question because the computer has proved that images are malleable, changeable, fluid. In movies, advertisements, TV shows, and magazines we are constantly exposed to images that have been created or changed by computers. As William Mitchell points out in his book *The Reconfigured Eye: Photography in the Post-Photographic Era*, we are experiencing a paradigm shift in how we define the nature of a photograph. The photograph is no longer a fixed image; it has become a composite of movable pixels, and this is changing how we perceive what a photograph is. The bottom line is that documentary photojournalism is the last vestige of real photography.

Journalists have only one thing to offer the public: credibility. Without it we have nothing. We might as well go sell widgets door to door, since without the trust of the public we cannot exist as a profession.

Our credibility is damaged every time a reputable news organization is caught lying to the public. One of the most blatant and widely recognized cases was the *Time* cover photo of O. J. Simpson. *Time* took the mug shot of Simpson when he was arrested and changed it for use on their cover. *Time* would not have been caught if *Newsweek* had not used the same photo on its cover the same week. The two covers showed up on the newsstands next to each other, and the public could see something that was wrong. *Time* had darkened the photo, creating a five o'clock shadow and a more sinister look. They had darkened the top of the photo and made the police line-up numbers smaller. They had decided Simpson was guilty, so they made him look guilty.

In an editorial the next week, *Time*'s managing editor said, "the photo was smoothed into an icon of tragedy." In other words, *Time* changed the photo from what it was (a document) into what they wanted it to be. *Time* was making an editorial statement, not reporting the news. They presented what looked like a real photograph, and it turned out not to be real; the public felt deceived—and rightly so. By doing this, *Time* damaged their credibility and the credibility of all journalists.

To have a rational, logical discussion of ethics, a distinction needs to be drawn between ethics and taste. Ethics refers to issues of deception or lying. Taste refers to issues involving blood, sex, violence, and other aspects of life that we probably do not want to see in our morning paper as we eat breakfast. Not everyone defines taste or ethics this way, but I find it useful. Issues of taste can cause a few subscription cancellations and letters to the editor, but they tend to evaporate in a few days. Ethics violations damage credibility, and the effects can last for years. Once you damage your credibility, it is next to impossible to get it back.

Publication of the photo of the dead American soldier being dragged through the streets of Mogadishu raises issues of taste, not issues of ethics. This photo is a fair and accurate representation of what happened in Somalia that day (I hesitate to use the word "truthful." Truth is a loaded concept, open to personal interpretation. What is true for one person might not be true for another. I prefer to use the terms "fair and accurate." These terms are more precise, though not completely without debate over their meaning.) If we are to use this photo, a photo that is ethically correct but definitely of questionable taste (no one wants to see dead American soldiers in the newspaper), we need to have a compelling reason. The principle that I find useful here is this: If the public needs the information in the photo to make informed choices for society, then we must run the photo. We cannot make informed choices for our society unless we have access to fair and accurate information. A free society is based on this right. It is codified in our country as the First Amendment to the Constitution. To make decisions that affect us as a society, we have to know what is happening in our towns, in our country, and in our world. The First Amendment does not belong to the press; it belongs to the American people. It guarantees all of us the right to the fair and accurate information we need to be responsible citizens.

We needed to see the dead soldier in the streets so that we could make an informed choice as a country as to the correctness of our being in Somalia. Words can tell us the facts, but photos hit us in the gut. They give us the real meaning, the deep and emotional impact of what was happening, much better than words can. As a society we chose to leave Somalia.

I feel badly for the family of the soldier, but sometimes the needs of the many outweigh the needs of the few—or the one. In our country we have the right to our privacy (the Sixth Amendment is usually cited), but we also have to live together and act collectively. This need is addressed by the First Amendment: "Congress shall make no law respecting an establishment of religion, or prohibiting the free exercise thereof; or abridging the freedom of speech or of the press; or the right of the people to peaceably assemble, and to petition the government for a redress of grievances."

Honest photographs can have an ethical dimension when it concerns the personal ethics of the photographer. Did the photographer violate some ethical standard in the process of making the picture?

For example, take the very famous photo of the young child dying in Africa while a vulture stands behind, waiting. It was taken by Kevin Carter, who won a Pulitzer Prize for the photo (which also raised a lot of money for relief agencies). He was criticized for not helping the child; he replied that relief workers were there to do that. After receiving his Pulitzer, Kevin Carter returned to Africa and committed suicide. He had a lot of problems in his life, but with the timing of the sequence of events, I cannot help thinking that there was a correlation between his inaction with the child and his suicide.

This is the kind of choice every journalist will face sometime in his or her career—maybe not in the extreme situation that Carter faced, but in some way, we all will be faced with the choice of helping or photographing. Some day you will be at a fire or a car accident, and you will be called on to put the camera down and help. It is a good idea to think about these issues in advance because when the hour comes, it will come suddenly, and you will be asked to make a choice quickly.

Here is the principle that works for me. It is not a popular one, and it is one that many journalists disagree with, but it allows me to sleep at night: If you have placed yourself in the position where you can help, you are morally obligated to help. I do not ask you to agree with me. I just want you to think about this and be prepared.

It is time to get back to a discussion on the ethics involved with the use of computers to process images.

Where the photo runs makes all the difference in the world. Let's take an obviously computer-enhanced photo, the kind you can find in the *Weekly World News*. If this same photo ran on the front page of the *New York Times*, it would damage the credibility of the *Times*. It cannot damage the credibility of the *Weekly World News* because that newspaper does not have any credibility to begin with. (It seems that we need to create a new set of terms when we can refer to both the *Weekly World News* and the *New York Times* as newspapers.)

Context becomes a problem when we find digitally altered photos in reputable publications, and there have been many. For example, the cover of *Texas Monthly* once ran a photo of then Governor Ann Richards astride a Harley Davidson motorcycle. It came out that the only part of the photo that was really Ann Richards was her head. The body on the motorcycle belonged to a model, and the head of the governor has been electronically attached to the model. The editors claimed that they explained on the credit page, in very small type, what they had done and that this disclosure exonerated them. However, this was buried on the bottom of a page that very few people read, in a type size that few over the age of 40 can read, and it was worded in such a way as to be incomprehensible. Furthermore, no amount of captioning can forgive a visual lie. In the context of news, if a photo looks real, it had better be real.

The *Texas Monthly* photo looked real, but it was a fake. We have an obligation to history to leave behind us a collection of real photographs. This photo of Ann Richards entered the public domain, and on the day she lost her reelection bid, AP ran the photo on the wire for its clients. AP had to run a mandatory kill when they were informed that it was not a real photo. You have to have the same respect for the visual image that you have for the written word. You do not lie with words, nor should you lie with photographs.

There are degrees of changes that can be done electronically to a photograph. There are technical changes that deal only with the aspects of photography that make the photo more readable, such as a little dodging and burning, global color correction, and contrast control. These are all part of the grammar of photography, just as there is a grammar associated with words (e.g., sentence structure, capital letters, paragraphs) that make it possible to read a story, so there is a grammar of photography that allows us to read a photograph. These changes (like their darkroom counterparts) are neither ethical nor unethical; they are merely technical.

More germane to ethical discussions, there are changes that are not technical but rather involve the content of a photo. Some changes are obviously more important than others. Some changes are just cosmetic (such as taking out telephone wires in the background of a photo), while some alter the basic content of the photo (such as putting a new head on someone else's body). Small changes might not change the meaning of a photo, but they are still lies. Little lies are lies nonetheless.

I do not think the public cares whether it is a little lie or a big lie. As far as they are concerned all lies are bad. Once the shutter has been tripped and the moment has been captured on film, in the context of news, we no longer have the right to change the content of the photo in any way. Any change to a news photo—any violation of that moment—is a lie. Big or small, any lie damages your credibility.

The reason I get so adamant when I discuss this issue is that the documentary photograph is a very powerful thing, and its power is based on the fact that it is real. The real photograph gives us a window on history; it allows us to be present at the great events of our times and the past. It gets its power from the fact that it represents exactly what the photographer saw through the medium of photography. The raw reality that it depicts, the verisimilitude, makes the documentary photo come alive. Look at the work of Robert Capa, or David Douglas Duncan, or the other great war photographers; look at the photo of Martin Luther King shot on the balcony of the Lorraine Motel. Their power comes from the fact they are real moments in time captured as they happened, unchanged. To change any detail in any of these photographs diminishes their power and turns them into lies. They would no longer be what the photographer saw but what someone else wanted the scene to be. The integrity of the moment would be destroyed in favor of the editorial concept being foisted, as occurred in the case of the *Time* cover photo of O. J. Simpson.

There have been many cases of digital manipulation over the past 20 years or so, the first of note being the famous pyramids cover of *National Geographic* in 1982. *National Geographic* had a horizontal photo of the pyramids in Egypt and wanted to make a vertical cover from it. They put the photo in a computer and squeezed the pyramids together—a difficult task in real life but an easy one for the computer. They referred to the process as the "retroactive repositioning of the photographer" (one of the great euphemisms of our age), saying that if the photographer had been a little to one side or the other, this is what he would have gotten. The photographer was not 10 feet to the right, and he did not get the photo they wanted, so they created a visual lie. They damaged their credibility, and although (as I said before) taste issues have a short life span, ethics issues do not go away. Here we are almost 20 years later, and we are still talking about what *National Geographic* did.

The list can go on for pages: *Newsweek* straightened the teeth of the woman who had the septuplets; *Newsday* ran a photo supposedly showing Nancy Kerrigan and Tonya Harding skating together before the event ever happened; *People* ran a photo of famous breast cancer survivors that was made from five separate negatives; the *St. Louis Post Dispatch* removed a Coke can from a photo of their Pulitzer Prize winner. This just scratches the surface. How many cases have not become known? The cumulative effect is a gradual erosion of the credibility of the entire profession, and I am not sure we can win. We are being bombarded from all sides—from movies, television, advertisements, and the Internet—with images that are not real, that are created in computers.

We may be in a struggle, but the end is worth fighting for. Real photos can change people's hearts and minds. Real photographs can change how we view war and how we view our society. Vietnam is a prime example of this. Two photos sum up that war: Nick Ut's photo of a crying girl running naked down a road away from her bombed village and Eddie Adams's photo of a man being executed on a Saigon street. These photos changed how we perceived that war. They are powerful, and they get their power from the fact that they are real moments captured for all time on film.

No one has the right to change these photos or the content of any documentary photo. We have an obligation to history to leave a fair and accurate record of our age

AREAS FOR DISCUSSION

- Do research and bring information about litigation involving the taking of visual content from a web site.
- Discuss the difference between taste and ethics.
- Outline and create your own personal code of ethics as an emerging professional photojournalist.

Additive primary colors. Red, green, and blue. The addition of red, green, and blue light produces white light. Blue and green make cyan; blue and red produce magenta; and red and green create yellow.

Analogue. Derived from *analogous*, meaning similar to something. Analogue tools convert real-world occurrences such as light and sound into electronic representations such as film or audiotape. Analogue is the opposite of digital, which converts real-world information into numbers: ones and zeros.

Archive. A copy of data files on disks, CD-ROM, or tape for long-term storage.

Array. A series of storage devices, typically hard disks, that work together as a single storage unit for providing continued access during crashes, disaster recovery, or increased throughput.

Bandwidth. Refers to the range of frequencies, expressed in hertz, capable of passing through a circuit.

Bit depth. The amount of colors or levels of gray that is displayed at one time. This is determined by the memory of a computer's graphics card. For example, a 16-bit card shows 64,000 colors.

Cache. Pronounced "cash." An allotment of high-speed memory that functions as a temporary storage area for frequently used data. Cache allows quicker retrieval of information as it eliminates the need to access the data from the original storage area.

Calibration. A measurement of the effects of an imaging process on a color/grayscale object.

CCD. Charged coupled device. The technology that forms the basis of most image acquisition products, such as scanners and digital cameras. The image becomes focused on an array of light-sensitive cells that reflects the light back as voltages.

CD. Compact disc. A standard storage device of digital data accessed by a laser-based reader.

CMYK. Cyan, magenta, yellow, and black. The four process colors of four-color printing. CMYK is also a color model used in desktop publishing, the others being HSB, PMS, and RGB.

Compression. A process that minimizes (shrinks) a file so that it takes up less storage space and allows for faster transmission. This process involves taking out blank data and replacing it with symbolic codes.

Copyright law. Legal protection of original expression (writing, music, visual art, etc.) from the moment it becomes tangible so that it may not be used by anyone other than the person or group who produced the expression. This protection extends to any image found on the web, regardless of any copyright notice posted by the creator.

Contrast. The range between an image's lightest and darkest tones.

Cropping. Trimming unwanted areas of an image.

Cyan. One of four colored inks used in the four-color printing process. It is a subtractive process color, reflecting blue and green while absorbing red.

Densitometer. A device that measures the density of a printed image and is frequently used to make sure colors are uniform during a press run.

Density. An image's degree of darkness as well as the percent of screen that an image uses.

Digital camera. A camera that reads visual information (light and dark) and transforms it into pixels. The camera then translates the pixels' light levels into numbers according to color.

Digital Hybrid System. The system used by many newspapers and publications of shooting film and then scanning to attain the resulting digital image file.

Digital information. Information recorded with binary code. This information can be text in a binary code form (e.g., ASCII), images that have been scanned in a bitmap form, digital sound, and video.

Dot gain. An occurrence during exposure and development of film or a plate when a halftone dot grows larger. It can also occur from the reaction between ink and paper. This enlargement must be compensated for in the prepress phase.

DPI. An abbreviation for dots per inch which defines output resolution for various media including traditional print or web publication.

EPS. Encapsulated PostScript. A file format that supports vector graphics and bitmap images.

Fair use. An ambiguous exception written into the U.S. Copyright Act that allows certain limited use of copyrighted materials under specific circumstances and for specific purposes.

File formats. Saving data in a configuration that is specific to the ultimate function of that data, such as text or graphics. JPEG and PICT are examples of graphic file formats.

FTP. File Transfer Protocol. A method for transferring data from a computer to or from an Internet server.

GIF. Graphics Interchange Format. A bitmap file format that provides modest compression capabilities.

Image resolution. A description in dots per inch (dpi) of an image's fineness or roughness after being digitized.

Internet. An interconnected, worldwide communication network that was originally developed by the U.S. federal government for linking government agencies with academic networks.

Interpolation. A process that averages pixel information as an image is scaled. Reducing the size of an image causes pixels to create a single, new pixel; conversely, enlarging an image causes the creation of additional pixels.

Intranet. A private, in-house version of the Internet for a company or organization.

JPEG. Joint Photographic Experts Group. A compression file format for photographic images in which nonessential image data is removed when the image file is compressed. The JPEG file format can support millions of colors.

Line screen. A halftone's resolution expressed as lines per inch.

Lossless compression (also see LZW). Image file compression format that preserves the original image without losing data when used to compress JPEG files.

Lossy compression. Image file compression format used to compress JPEG image files that can lose image data when compressing a file.

LZW. Lempel-Ziv-Welch. A lossless data compression algorithm that is used to create GIF file formats.

Modes in Photoshop. Settings contained in the Options palette used with painting and editing tools. These modes control which pixels are affected when painting or editing, depending on the tool's opacity, pressure, or fade-out settings.

Noise. Undesirable artifacts that can appear on an image from specks, gray areas, visible handwritten lines, and the like.

Plug-in. Additional software application that adds different functionality to specific programs.

PNG. Portable Network Graphic. A file format that compresses.

Prepress. The preparation required for making camera-ready artwork into printing plates used for mass production.

Public domain. Material that is usable by anyone (e.g., government documents) or material that has passed from being protected by copyright into something that anyone can use. Copyright protection extends to the lifetime of the creator plus 70 years.

RAM. Random access memory. A computer's primary memory, which is accessed quicker than any other form of memory storage device.

Resolution. The measure of a printer's output capability, expressed typically in dots per inch (dpi). Also, the measure of a halftone's quality, expressed typically in lines per inch.

RGB. Red, Green, Blue. The additive primary colors of color TV screens and monitors. Combined, these three colors represent the entire color spectrum.

Scanner. An instrument that optically senses an image and uses software to transfer the image's information into machine-readable code.

SCSI. Pronounced "scuzzy." Small Computer System Interface. This is an industry standard device used for connecting peripheral equipment, such as scanners, hard disks, and tape drives, to a microprocessor.

Slug. A short word or term that is used to label a photo or story when filing or archiving for later reference.

Subtractive primary colors. Cyan, magenta, and yellow. They are called subtractive because of their use as pigment, dye, or another colorant in subtracting from or filtering white light into a certain hue.

TIFF. Tagged Image Extraction technology. A bitmap file format that describes and stores color and grayscale images.

Virtual memory. A portion of a computer's hard disk space that is used as "fake" memory. The user can intentionally increase the amount of hard disk space used for virtual memory.

Zip drive/disk. A storage drive that is either built into a computer or attached separately and is used for Zip disks, a popular form of data storage with a large capacity.

NOTES

NOTES

NOTES